# Strategic READING 3
## Building Effective Reading Skills

**Student's Book**

**CAMBRIDGE**
UNIVERSITY PRESS

Jack C. Richards    Samuela Eckstut-Didier

CAMBRIDGE UNIVERSITY PRESS
Cambridge, New York, Melbourne, Madrid, Cape Town, Singapore, São Paulo

Cambridge University Press
40 West 20th Street, New York, NY 10011-4211, USA

www.cambridge.org
Information on this title: www.cambridge.org/9780521555784

First published 2003
2nd printing 2005

Printed in Hong Kong, China

A catalog record for this publication is available from the British Library

ISBN-13   978-0-521-55578-4 student's book
ISBN-10   0-521-55578-7 student's book

ISBN-13   978-0-521-55575-3 teacher's manual
ISBN-10   0-521-55575-2 teacher's manual

Art direction, book design, and layout services: Adventure House, NYC

# Contents

| | | |
|---|---|---|
| **Authors' Acknowledgments** | | **v** |
| **Scope and sequence** | | **vi** |
| **Introduction** | | **x** |

**UNIT 1** **Superstitions** **1**

Two worlds 2
Lucky hats and other fishing superstitions 4
A superstition about new calendars 6

**UNIT 2** **Health** **9**

Diets of the world 10
Drink, blink, and rest 12
Azeri hills hold secret of long life 14

**UNIT 3** **Talent** **17**

A prodigy in mother's eyes 18
Born to paint 20
The sound of silence 22

**UNIT 4** **Beauty** **25**

Executives go under the knife 26
What makes a man attractive? 28
In the land of the mirror 30

**UNIT 5** **Technology** **33**

The car that thinks it's your friend 34
Identification, please! 36
Researchers worry as teens grow up online 38

**UNIT 6** **Punishment** **41**

Spanking on trial 42
The Letter 44
Schools take the fun out of suspension 46

**UNIT 7** **Loss** **49**

Death & superstition 50
Chapter Two 52
Funeral Blues; The Chariot 54

| UNIT 8 | **Memory** | **57** |
| | Can you believe what you see? | 58 |
| | Man weds the wife he forgot | 60 |
| | Repeat after me: Memory takes practice | 62 |

| UNIT 9 | **Personality** | **65** |
| | What do our possessions say about us? | 66 |
| | The role of temperament in shaping individuality | 68 |
| | Mind your P's and Q's | 70 |

| UNIT 10 | **Celebrity** | **73** |
| | I'm just another kid from Brooklyn | 74 |
| | California law has paparazzi shuddering | 76 |
| | Fan club confessions | 78 |

| UNIT 11 | **The circus** | **81** |
| | Getting serious about clowning | 82 |
| | Circus town | 84 |
| | Tragedy at the circus; Circus safe for animals | 86 |

| UNIT 12 | **Martial arts** | **89** |
| | Shaolin Temple | 90 |
| | The karate generation | 92 |
| | Iron and silk | 94 |

| UNIT 13 | **Fashion** | **97** |
| | Smart clothes | 98 |
| | It's a dog's life | 100 |
| | How to separate trends from fads | 102 |

| UNIT 14 | **The media** | **105** |
| | Something strange is happening to tabloids | 106 |
| | When our worlds collide | 108 |
| | Media violence harms children; Media violence does not harm children | 110 |

| UNIT 15 | **Art** | **113** |
| | Girl with a Pitcher | 114 |
| | Organic architecture | 116 |
| | How forgeries corrupt our museums | 118 |

| UNIT 16 | **Humor** | **121** |
| | So, who's the comedian? | 122 |
| | Taking humor seriously in the workplace | 124 |
| | Three comedians | 126 |

# Authors' Acknowledgments

The publisher would like to thank the following **reviewers** for their helpful insights and suggestions in the development of the series: Orlando Carranza, Ann Conable, Elliot Judd, Madeleine Kim, Laura LeDréan, Laura MacGregor, Sandy Soghikian, Colleen Weldele, and Junko Yamanaka.

We would also like to acknowledge the **students** and **teachers** in the following schools and institutes who piloted materials in the initial development stages:

**Associação Alumni**, São Paulo, Brazil; **AUA Language Center**, Bangkok, Thailand; **Case Western Reserve University**, Cleveland, Ohio, USA; **Hokusei Gakuen University**, Sapporo, Japan; **Hunter College**, New York, New York, USA; **Instituto Brasil-Estados Unidos (IBEU)**, Rio de Janeiro, Brazil; **Instituto Cultural Peruano Norteamericano**, Lima, Peru; **Kyung Hee University**, Seoul, Korea; **Miyagi Gakuin Women's College**, Miyagi, Japan; **Queens College**, Flushing, New York, USA; **Sapporo International University**, Sapporo, Japan.

We also would like to thank the many additional schools in the above countries whose students responded to surveys on their reading interests and preferences.

A special thanks to Lynn Bonesteel and Robert L. Maguire for their invaluable advice and support. The authors are also grateful to Chuck Sandy for his contribution to the early development of the project.

Thanks also go to the **editorial** and **production** team: Eleanor Barnes, Sylvia Bloch, David Bohlke, Karen Davy, Tünde Dewey, Anne Garrett, Deborah Goldblatt, Nada Gordon, Louisa Hellegers, Lise Minovitz, Diana Nam, Bill Paulk, Mary Sandre, Howard Siegelman, Jane Sturtevant, Kayo Taguchi, and Louisa van Houten.

Finally, special thanks to Cambridge University Press **staff** and **advisors**: Jim Anderson, Mary Louise Baez, Carlos Barbisan, Kathleen Corley, Kate Cory-Wright, Riitta da Costa, Elizabeth Fuzikava, Steve Golden, Yuri Hara, Gareth Knight, Andy Martin, Nigel McQuitty, Mark O'Neil, Dan Schulte, Catherine Shih, Su-Wei Wang, and Ellen Zlotnick.

# Scope and sequence

| Unit | Readings | Skills | Vocabulary |
|---|---|---|---|
| **Unit 1**<br>**Superstitions** | Two worlds<br><br>Lucky hats and other fishing superstitions<br><br>A supersition about new calendars | Guessing meaning from context<br>Making inferences<br>Predicting<br>Scanning<br>Understanding details<br>Understanding text organization | Superstition-related terms<br>Luck idioms |
| **Unit 2**<br>**Health** | Diets of the world<br><br>Drink, blink and rest<br><br>Azeri hills hold secret of long life | Guessing meaning from context<br>Predicting<br>Recognizing similarity in meaning<br>Recognizing tone<br>Scanning<br>Understanding details<br>Understanding main ideas<br>Understanding reference words | Medical terms<br>Dictionary abbreviations |
| **Unit 3**<br>**Talent** | A prodigy in mother's eyes<br><br>Born to paint<br><br>The sound of silence | Guessing meaning from context<br>Making inferences<br>Predicting<br>Recognizing sources<br>Scanning<br>Understanding main ideas | Talent-related terms<br>Phrasal verbs |
| **Unit 4**<br>**Beauty** | Executives go under the knife<br><br>What makes a man attractive?<br><br>In the land of the mirror | Guessing meaning from context<br>Predicting<br>Recognizing purpose<br>Scanning<br>Understanding details<br>Understanding reference words<br>Understanding text organization | Adjectives (beauty)<br>Descriptions of facial features |

| Unit | Readings | Skills | Vocabulary |
|------|----------|--------|------------|
| **Unit 5**<br>**Technology** | The car that thinks it's your friend<br><br>Information, please!<br><br>Researchers worry as teens grow up online | Guessing meaning from context<br>Predicting<br>Recognizing purpose<br>Restating and making inferences<br>Scanning<br>Understanding details | Computer terms<br>Car-related terms<br>Internet shorthand |
| **Unit 6**<br>**Punishment** | Spanking on trial<br><br>The Letter<br><br>Schools take the fun out of suspension | Guessing meaning from context<br>Making inferences<br>Predicting<br>Recognizing point of view<br>Recognizing purpose<br>Recognizing tone<br>Scanning<br>Understanding reference words<br>Understanding text organization | Punishment-related terms<br>Crimes<br>Parts of speech |
| **Unit 7**<br>**Loss** | Death & superstition<br><br>Chapter Two<br><br>Funeral Blues; The Chariot | Guessing meaning from context<br>Making inferences<br>Predicting<br>Recognizing similarity in meaning<br>Rhyming<br>Scanning<br>Skimming<br>Understanding details<br>Understanding main ideas | Funeral customs<br>Homographs |
| **Unit 8**<br>**Memory** | Can you believe what you see?<br><br>Man weds the wife he forgot<br><br>Repeat after me: Memory takes practice | Distinguishing main and supporting ideas<br>Guessing meaning from context<br>Predicting<br>Scanning<br>Understanding details<br>Understanding reference words | Memory-related terms<br>Memory idioms |

| Unit | Readings | Skills | Vocabulary |
|------|----------|--------|------------|
| **Unit 9**<br>**Personality** | What do our possessions say about us?<br><br>The role of temperament in shaping individuality<br><br>Mind your P's and Q's | Guessing meaning from context<br>Predicting<br>Recognizing similarity in meaning<br>Recognizing sources<br>Restating and making inferences<br>Scanning<br>Understanding main ideas<br>Understanding details | Adjectives (personality) |
| **Unit 10**<br>**Celebrity** | I'm just another kid from Brooklyn<br><br>California law has paparazzi shuddering<br><br>Fan club confessions | Distinguishing arguments<br>Guessing meaning from context<br>Making restatements<br>Predicting<br>Recognizing audience<br>Scanning<br>Skimming<br>Understanding details<br>Understanding main ideas | Celebrity-related terms<br>Prefix *out-* |
| **Unit 11**<br>**The circus** | Getting serious about clowning<br><br>Circus town<br><br>Tragedy at the circus; Circus safe for animals | Distinguishing arguments<br>Distinguishing fact from opinion<br>Guessing meaning from context<br>Predicting<br>Recognizing similarity in meaning<br>Scanning<br>Understanding details<br>Understanding main ideas | Circus-related terms<br>Phrasal verbs |
| **Unit 12**<br>**Martial arts** | Shaolin Temple<br><br>The karate generation<br><br>Iron and Silk | Guessing meaning from context<br>Making inferences<br>Predicting<br>Recognizing sources<br>Scanning<br>Understanding details<br>Understanding main ideas<br>Understanding text organization | Martial arts terms<br>Prefix *self-* |

| Unit | Readings | Skills | Vocabulary |
|------|----------|--------|------------|
| **Unit 13**<br>**Fashion** | Smart clothes<br><br>It's a dog's life<br><br>How to separate trends from fads | Guessing meaning from context<br>Recognizing audience<br>Scanning<br>Understanding complex sentences<br>Understanding details<br>Restating | Fashion-related terms<br>Acronyms |
| **Unit 14**<br>**The media** | Something stange is happening to tabloids<br><br>When our worlds collide<br><br>Media violence harms children; Media violence does not harm children | Guessing meaning from context<br>Making inferences<br>Predicting<br>Restating<br>Scanning<br>Skimming<br>Understanding complex sentences<br>Understanding main ideas | Media-related terms<br>Prefixes *counter-*, *mis-*, and *inter-* |
| **Unit 15**<br>**Art** | Girl with a Pitcher<br><br>Organic architecture<br><br>How forgeries corrupt our museums | Guessing meaning from context<br>Making inferences<br>Predicting<br>Recognizing sources<br>Recognizing tone<br>Scanning<br>Understanding complex sentences<br>Understanding details<br>Understanding reference words | Art, architecture and museum terms<br>Compound adjectives |
| **Unit 16**<br>**Humor** | So, who's the comedian?<br><br>Taking humor seriously in the workplace<br><br>Three comedians | Guessing meaning from context<br>Making inferences<br>Predicting<br>Recognizing similarity in meaning<br>Recognizing tone<br>Restating<br>Scanning<br>Skimming<br>Understanding details | Performance-related terms<br>Humor-related idioms |

# Introduction

## Overview

*Strategic Reading* features texts from a variety of authentic sources, including newspapers, magazines, books, and websites. The texts, which have been adapted for level appropriateness, allow students to build essential reading skills while they examine important topics in their lives.

*Strategic Reading 3* is designed to develop the reading, vocabulary-building, and critical thinking skills of young-adult and adult learners of English at an intermediate to high-intermediate level.

## Format

Each book in the *Strategic Reading* series contains 16 units divided into three readings on a particular theme. Every unit includes the sections described below:

### Preview

The units begin with brief descriptions previewing the readings in the unit. These descriptions are accompanied by discussion questions designed to stimulate student interest and activate background knowledge on the theme.

This page also introduces some of the vocabulary found in the readings. These words and phrases are recycled throughout the unit to provide students with many opportunities to process and internalize new vocabulary.

### Readings

Different genres of readings have been gathered from novels, plays, magazines, textbooks, websites, poetry, newspapers, and editorials to reflect realistically the varied nature of the written world. These texts increase gradually in length and difficulty as students progress through the book. A full page of challenging exercises, divided into the following three sets of activities, focuses students on each reading.

#### Before you read

This section encourages students to think more carefully about a specific area of the theme. When students make predictions based on their personal experiences, a valuable link between background knowledge and new information is formed.

**Reading**

One *Skimming* or *Scanning* activity accompanies every reading in the book. In this section, students must either skim or scan a passage to look for specific information or to confirm predictions made in the pre-reading activity. After, students are instructed to read the whole text.

**After you read**

The exercises in this section concentrate on the following reading skills (see the Scope and sequence chart on pages vi–ix) developed throughout the book:

- understanding main ideas and details;

- making inferences and guessing meaning from context;

- understanding the organization and cohesion of a text;

- recognizing an audience, source, tone, or point of view;

- distinguishing fact from opinion; and

- understanding complex sentences and the sequence of events.

In order to focus on multiple skills and accommodate different learning and teaching styles, a wide variety of task types are featured in these exercises. These task types include multiple choice, matching, true/false, and fill in the blank. These varied activities are designed to practice all aspects of a particular skill, and to maintain the interest of both students and teachers.

Each reading ends with an exercise called *Relating reading to personal experience* that allows students to use vocabulary introduced in the unit to share their thoughts, opinions, and experiences in writing or in discussions.

## Wrap-up

Every unit ends with a one-page review section where students apply and expand their knowledge of unit vocabulary to complete a variety of fun and challenging word games and puzzles.

As a final activity, students work on a project or participate in a discussion related to the unit theme. Activities such as designing and conducting surveys, researching and presenting information, and interviewing others provide meaningful closure to the unit.

*Strategic Reading 3* is accompanied by a Teacher's Manual that contains a model lesson plan, definitions of key vocabulary, comprehensive teaching suggestions, cultural notes, unit quizzes, and answers to activities and quizzes.

# UNIT 1 Superstitions

**You are going to read three texts about superstitions. First, answer the questions in the boxes.**

## Two worlds

Read an excerpt from a memoir about childhood fascination with tales of superstition.

1. Who used to tell you stories when you were a child?
2. Have you ever had your fortune told? If so, did any predictions come true?
3. Do you know someone who is superstitious? Do you think this person is rational?

## Lucky hats and other fishing superstitions

What are common superstitions among fishermen? The writer of this newspaper article talks about some of them.

1. Do you like to go fishing? If so, how often do you go?
2. What equipment do you need to go fishing?
3. Do you think you need luck to succeed in fishing? Why or why not?

## A superstition about new calendars

The writer of this newspaper article describes some problems caused by one of his childhood superstitions.

1. What do you like most about the New Year?
2. What traditions do you follow on New Year's Day?
3. Do you know any superstitions associated with New Year's Day?

## Vocabulary

**To find out the meanings of the words in the box, work with another student, ask your teacher, or use a dictionary. Then circle the words that you associate with superstitions.**

| | | | |
|---|---|---|---|
| a boogeyman | a miracle | a prognostication | a saint |
| a curse | the evil eye | roots and herbs | souls of the dead |

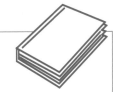

# Two worlds

*In this autobiographical excerpt about her childhood in Peru, Gabriella de Ferrari writes about how her mother, her neighbor Señorita Luisa, and her maid Saturnina look at the world.*

1     Early in life I realized that there were two very different ways of looking at the world, my parents' and Señorita Luisa's. What she told me was what I assumed the world outside my house believed. At home what I was told was what people believed in that faraway place where my parents came from. I kept them separate and functioned accordingly, never suffering from the difference, at least while I was young and the lines were so easy to draw. Yet Señorita Luisa's world, together with that of the maids in the kitchen, was far more seductive than the rational world of my parents. I liked curses and miracles, and praying for a handsome husband, and buying up heaven.

2     Mother and Señorita Luisa talked to each other constantly. They would sit under a large mulberry tree in the afternoon and become absorbed in each other's stories. My own time with Señorita Luisa came in the evenings, when I got back from school. I would go to her house for a snack of hot chocolate and a cake she made especially for me of fresh figs held together with what she called "honey glue." She had many stories to tell, and they were all equally outrageous. I listened, mesmerized by her tales delivered in the monotonous rhythms of her voice as if they occurred every day, like drinking milk or taking a bath.

3     One of my favorite activities, in which Señorita Luisa would indulge me only when she was in a good mood, was to have my fortune read. She would drip hot wax from a candle into a large container of icy water. When the wax hit the water, it formed different shapes. She read them and told me my "little future," that is, my future for the next week. The prognostications were mostly designed to teach me to behave: "This week you will tell a lie and that will cost you, because your mother will not believe you anymore." Only occasionally would she tell me my "big future," the one I wanted to hear the most: A handsome man would fall in love with me, a man with green eyes and dark hair like Luisa's brothers.

4     The maids in my family's kitchen were also constantly reading wax, but they weren't allowed to read wax for me. My mother thought it was nonsense. She never knew that Señorita Luisa read my fortune. Señorita Luisa also told ghost stories about the *almas*, the souls of the dead that came to visit at night. She used to scare me so much I had to ask Saturnina to stay with me until I fell asleep. Saturnina knew how to send the souls away: She tied a black ribbon to the window and left them a piece of bread.

5     As Señorita Luisa had saints, Saturnina and the other maids had roots and herbs. These could perform any kind of miracle, especially scaring away the "evil eye" that women gave each other when they were interested in the same man. I was constantly torn between wanting to believe Señorita Luisa and Saturnina and wanting to believe Mother, who was more interested in having me worry about geography and math.

**READING TIP**   Scan the text to understand important details. Read quickly to look for information that answers a specific question, such as the names of characters or important words and phrases.

Adapted from *Gringa Latina*.

## Before you read

**Look at these sentences from the text. Then check (✓) the statement that you think will be the main idea of the text.**

. . . there were two very different ways of looking at the world, my parents' and Señorita Luisa's.
One of my favorite activities . . . was to have my fortune read.
The maids . . . were constantly reading wax, but they weren't allowed to read wax for me.

_____ 1. The writer's mother paid Señorita Luisa to teach her daughter about superstitions, something that every young girl should learn.
_____ 2. As a child, the writer loved being with the maids and Señorita Luisa more than she liked being with her parents.
_____ 3. As a child, the writer lived in a world where many people believed in superstitions, but her parents didn't.

## Reading

**Scan the text to check your prediction. Then read the whole text.**

## After you read

**A** **Find the words in *italics* in the reading. Circle the meaning of each word.**

1. When something is *seductive,* it is **attractive** / **frightening** / **painful**. (par. 1)
2. When something is *outrageous,* it **is very unusual and surprising** / **happens outside** / **makes people feel sad**. (par. 2)
3. When something *mesmerizes* you, it is **boring** / **interesting** / **confusing**. (par. 2)
4. When people *indulge* you, they do something you **need** / **don't want** / **want**. (par. 3)
5. When you think something is *nonsense,* you don't **understand it** / **think it will happen** / **think it's reasonable**. (par. 4)

**B** **Check (✔) the statements that are true.**

___✓___ 1. Saturnina worked for the writer's family.

_____ 2. Señorita Luisa worked for the writer's family.

_____ 3. Señorita Luisa and the writer's mother were friends.

_____ 4. The writer's parents were born in a foreign country.

_____ 5. The writer's mother would be pleased that Saturnina had read wax for her.

_____ 6. Unlike Señorita Luisa, the writer's mother wasn't superstitious.

**C** **Answer these questions.**

1. Would you like to go to a fortune-teller? If so, what would you like to hear?

2. Do you believe in ghosts? If so, have you had any experiences with them?

3. Were you more or less superstitious as a child than you are now? Do you still believe in superstitions? If so, which ones?

# Lucky hats and other fishing superstitions

1 Last January, I was fortunate enough to go to Brazil on a fishing trip. As we were boarding the vessel that would be our home for the next six nights, I looked up and saw a huge bunch of ripe bananas hanging from a hook.

2 I was horrified. For more than 20 years, I have been told again and again that bananas and boats just don't mix. I started talking about it with my fishing companions. Not one had ever heard of such a superstition.

3 Yet just a few months earlier, I had read a paper about the banana superstition. The author was unable to find its origin. One bit of speculation is that dangerous critters lurked inside the banana bunches. But there's no doubt that anglers throughout the world believe that bananas don't mix with fishing boats.

4 The bananas certainly didn't affect the fishing in Brazil. They were downright tasty and the fishing was outstanding. But it got me to thinking about other superstitions regarding fishing.

5 For example, lucky hats. I had a lucky hat for a long time, a bright red cap that I was convinced was lucky. I caught a lot of fish and a lot of big fish wearing that hat. Then one day while angry, I threw it overboard. I'm convinced I haven't caught as many fish since.

6 Recently, a friend e-mailed me a list of "10 Fishing Superstitions" that appeared in a magazine. The lucky hat issue was addressed along with bananas. It says: "The 'right' hat can make or break a fishing

trip, but it can't be one you bought yourself." Hmmm. Come to think of it, that lucky cap of mine was a freebie.

7 There also were some I'd never heard of. For example, rabbits crossing your path were bad luck. Having a pig (or ham) on board is bad luck and so are eggs.

8 One superstition we've all heard is that it's good luck to spit on your bait; but this particular list suggests that if the bait is a fish, you should kiss it. Actually, the spitting on the bait probably has some merit. Just like a spray-on fish attractant, it can help disguise a smell that fish might find offensive.

9 There's also some merit in keeping the first fish you catch. Sheepshead fishermen, for example, don't like to release their fish until they prepare to leave an area because it will scare the rest of the school.

10 I have a good friend who is convinced that he won't catch any fish unless he first spills a soft drink in his boat. You can't just pour the drink out; it has to be done accidentally. That means you need to leave the drink in a precarious position when you put it down.

11 There are other superstitions as well. If you catch a fish on the first cast, you might as well go home; it will be the only fish you will catch. Cameras are bad luck. (That's really tough for me.)

12 I'm sure there are plenty more superstitions out there and I'd love to hear them. Let me know and I'll pass them along somewhere down the line. And remember, no bananas.

Adapted from *The Post and Courier*.

## Before you read

**Do you think these events are good luck or bad luck for fishermen?**
**Check (✓) the correct column.**

|  | Good Luck | Bad Luck |
|---|---|---|
| 1. Having bananas on a boat |  |  |
| 2. Having a pig (or ham) on a boat |  |  |
| 3. Having eggs on a boat |  |  |
| 4. Spitting on bait |  |  |
| 5. Spilling a soft drink on a boat |  |  |
| 6. Catching a fish on the first cast |  |  |

## Reading

**Scan the text to check your predictions. Then read the whole text.**

## After you read

**A** **Find the words and phrases in the reading that match these definitions.**
**Write one word on each line.**

1. getting on a boat     _boarding_    _a_    _vessel_ (par. 1)
2. insects or animals hid                    (par. 3)
3. fishermen                (par. 3)
4. something you get for free            (par. 6)
5. benefit or advantage            (par. 8 & 9)
6. hide something            (par. 8)
7. a large group of fish            (par. 9)
8. not safe or stable            (par. 10)

**B** **Check (✓) the correct column.**

| The writer's feelings about | Positive | Negative | Neutral |
|---|---|---|---|
| 1. ripe bananas on a boat |  | ✓ |  |
| 2. his fishing trip in Brazil |  |  |  |
| 3. his red cap |  |  |  |
| 4. rabbits crossing his path |  |  |  |
| 5. spitting on bait |  |  |  |
| 6. not taking photographs on a boat |  |  |  |

**C** **Answer these questions.**

1. Do you know any other superstitions associated with fishing (or other sports)?
   If so, what are they?
2. Do you have a lucky hat (or other article of clothing)? If so, where did you get it?
   Why do you consider it lucky?
3. Who do you think is more superstitious – men or women? What examples can you give?

# A superstition about new calendars

1 Don't forget to throw that quarter into your pot of black-eyed peas tomorrow . . . for good luck, of course.

2 I picked up my share of superstitions growing up, and several of them are connected with the New Year. The pot of peas seems more tradition to me than superstition, and it's easy to ignore since I don't cook. I can also say that another southern superstition – making sure a man is the first person to cross the threshold of your home on New Year's Day – also has no impact on my adult life. But one superstition I can't seem to escape is the one dealing with calendars. In my family, we believe it's bad luck to look at a new calendar before the start of the new year.

3 I can't ignore this because efficient administrative assistants at work hand out new calendars in late November or early December. And some of my co-workers hang them up as soon as they get them. So at any time, I'm likely to walk into a colleague's space and confront the offending object. If I see one, I avert my eyes. Try as I might to rid myself of this superstition, I'm not willing to take any chances, either.

4 I go through the same contortions each December. What to do if I see a new calendar? How do I avert my eyes while still preserving the air of a pragmatic professional? Sometimes it isn't easy.

5 I've found myself looking at the floor while talking with colleagues

or studiously examining a spot on the wall far away from a new calendar. As yet, none of my co-workers has called me on my seeming aloofness.

6 This December when the administrative aide at work asked if I wanted a calendar for next year, I didn't immediately say no as I usually do. I didn't say yes, either, but finally decided to rid myself of this silliness. So I did what any confident, competent adult does when confronted with a boogeyman of the past – I called my mother.

7 "Do you remember that superstition we had about putting a quarter in the black-eyed peas on New Year's Day?" I asked her.

8 "Well, it wasn't exactly a superstition," she said. "We did it for you kids. We wanted y'all to eat the peas, and maybe finding a

quarter in your plate was just a way to get you to do it."

9 "You mean you were trying to bribe us to eat?" I asked incredulously.

10 "What about calendars?" I asked, finally getting to the point of my telephone call. "Have you ever heard that it's bad luck to look at a calendar before the New Year?"

11 "Not to look at it but to hang it," she replied. "It's bad luck to hang a new calendar before the New Year."

12 There it was. I had remembered my superstition wrong. My contortions were all for nothing. No more staring at my feet in the face of a new calendar. Looking at one wouldn't bring me bad luck. My co-workers who hung the calendars were going to have the bad luck!

Adapted from *The Washington Post.*

## Before you read

dicting

**Look at these sentences from the text. Find out the meanings of any words you
don't know. Then answer the question in the box.**

1. . . . administrative assistants at work hand out new calendars in late November
   or early December.
2. . . . I'm likely to walk into a colleague's space and confront the offending object.
3. I go through the same contortions each December.
4. How do I avert my eyes while still preserving the air of a pragmatic professional?

What do you think the writer's superstition is?

## Reading

anning

**Scan the text to check your prediction. Then read the whole text.**

## After you read

derstanding
tails

**A** **Mark each sentence true (*T*) or false (*F*). Then correct the false sentences.**

   *throw a quarter into a pot of*
  _*F*_ 1. The children in the writer's family used to ~~eat~~ black-eyed peas for good luck.

  _____ 2. The writer thought that if a man were the first to enter the home on New
      Year's Day, the family would have good luck.

  _____ 3. The writer thought that if he waited until January to hang up a new
      calendar, he wouldn't have bad luck.

  _____ 4. If colleagues were sitting near a new calendar, the writer would not look at
      the people while talking to them.

  _____ 5. The writer called his mother to put an end to his superstition.

  _____ 6. The actual superstition was not to look at a calendar before the New Year.

nderstanding
xt
ganization

**B** **Which paragraphs in the text could these paragraphs follow? Write the numbers.**

  _____ a. "What about having a man be the first person in your house on New Year's
      Day?" I asked. "That's something I never believed in, but my grandmother
      wouldn't let a woman into her house on New Year's Day until a man had
      entered," my mother said. "She said she didn't want any woman bringing
      bad luck into her house at the start of the year. She was from the country
      and didn't know any better, though."

  _____ b. But now I wonder what other superstitions I picked up as a kid had been
      misunderstood. Then I remember something else I had learned very early –
      that my mother is always right. Hmmm.

elating
ading to
ersonal
xperience

**C** **Answer these questions.**

1. Do you know any holiday superstitions? If so, what are they?
2. Do you still believe any superstitions that you think are silly? If so, what are they?
3. Did your parents ever bribe you to do something? Do you think this is something
   parents should do? Why or why not?

## Vocabulary expansion

**A** Mark each expression positive in meaning (+) or negative in meaning (–).

___–___ 1. *be down on your luck*: suffer because bad things are happening to you

_____ 2. *be in luck*: get what you want

_____ 3. *be out of luck*: not get what you want

_____ 4. *better luck next time*: said to make someone feel better after something bad has happened

_____ 5. *bring someone luck*: make good things happen for someone

_____ 6. *just my luck*: said when something bad happens to you and you are not surprised

_____ 7. *luck out*: have something good happen to you by chance

_____ 8. *wish someone luck*: tell someone you hope he or she succeeds

_____ 9. *with my luck*: said when you think something bad will happen because you have bad luck

**B** Circle the correct words.

1. He's been down on his luck recently. He's **gotten** / **lost** two jobs in the past six months.
2. You're in luck. There are **no** / **some** tickets left for the concert.
3. You're out of luck. The sale **ended** / **started** yesterday.
4. **Too bad you lost.** / **I'm so glad you won.** Better luck next time!
5. Just my luck! I went on a picnic yesterday and **the weather was beautiful** / **it started to rain**.
6. I **always** / **never** wear this ring my grandfather gave me. It brings me luck.
7. He lucked out. He **got** / **didn't get** the job he wanted.
8. Wish me luck. I **am going to take** / **took** my driving test.
9. With my luck, the test will be really **easy** / **hard**.

## Superstitions and you

Work in pairs. What are some common superstitions? Make a list of at least five superstitions. Then compare lists as a class.

UNIT

# 2 Health

You are going to read three texts about health. First, answer the questions in the boxes.

**READING 1**

## Diets of the world

Read from this website to find out why people from some countries suffer fewer diet-related illnesses.

1. What do you typically eat every day? What do you avoid eating?
2. What types of food are associated with Chinese, French, and Mediterranean diets?
3. What medical problems can result from unhealthy eating?

**READING 2**

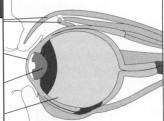

## Drink, blink, and rest

This magazine article offers tips to help keep your eyes healthy.

1. Do you wear glasses or contact lenses?
2. How many hours a day do you spend in front of a television and/or computer screen?
3. In the past few years, has your eyesight changed? If so, how?

**READING 3**

## Azeri hills hold secret of long life

This magazine article reveals why an unusual number of people in Azerbaijan live to be over 100 years old.

1. What do you know about Azerbaijan?
2. What is the average life expectancy of men in your country? What about women?
3. What factors lead to long life?

## Vocabulary

Find out the meanings of the words and phrases in the box. Then write each word or phrase next to the correct treatment.

| | | | | |
|---|---|---|---|---|
| an allergy | a cataract | a hacking cough | high blood pressure | a kidney stone |
| cancer | diabetes | heart disease | an infection | obesity |

Medication: _____

Surgery: _____

Medication and surgery: _____

# Diets of the world

1 Why do people in Asia get a fraction of the cancer, heart disease, and diabetes that Americans get? Why are the French, with their rich sauces, so slim? The secret may simmer in their food. For intense flavor and a healthier body, come visit these diets of the world.

## The Chinese diet

2 For centuries, the traditional Chinese diet has been primarily vegetarian – featuring lots of vegetables, rice, and soybeans – and containing only shavings of meat for flavoring. This is far healthier than the traditional American diet, which often features meat as the focus of the meal.

3 The traditional Chinese diet consists mainly of plant foods, small amounts of fish and poultry, and only occasionally red meat, says T. Colin Campbell, professor of nutrition at Cornell University. He has been comparing the diets in the United States and rural China by tracking the eating habits of people living in 100 Chinese rural villages. According to Campbell's research, the traditional Chinese diet is comprised of only 20 percent animal foods – far less than the amount in the typical American diet.

## The French diet

4 Flaky croissants, frogs' legs swimming in butter, and chocolate mousse: Despite their rich diet, the French are generally slimmer than Americans. According to research, just 8 percent of the French qualify as obese, compared to 33 percent of Americans. How do the French do it? The French tend to snack less and savor their meals more slowly – which could lead to eating less food overall.

5 The eating patterns of the French offer significant clues to their healthfulness. For one, they traditionally don't take lunch lightly. In a study that tracked the eating habits of 50 workers in Paris and Boston, the French participants consumed 60 percent of their day's calories before 2 P.M., followed later by a small dinner, so they were less likely to sleep after eating major calories. Secondly, the study found that the French participants didn't snack, generally defined as consuming one to two between-meal foods. "The French ate less than one snack a day. Here in the United States, we have about three snacks a day," says R. Curtis Ellison, professor of preventive medicine at Boston University.

## The Mediterranean diet

6 Ask Ancel Keys, 96, the secret of his long life, and he's likely to point to tonight's meal: baked cod flavored with lemon juice and olive oil, steamed broccoli, and roasted potatoes.

7 It's quintessentially Mediterranean, befitting the man who first promoted the health benefits of the Mediterranean diet. As a young scientist more than 50 years ago, Keys showed that among people in countries where fresh fruits and vegetables are plentiful and olive oil flows freely – Greece, southern Italy, southern France, parts of North Africa and the Middle East – heart disease is rare. In countries where people fill their plates with beef, cheese, and other foods high in saturated fat – like the United States – it's a leading cause of death.

8 The original Mediterranean diet, eaten by rural villagers on the Greek island of Crete, ". . . was nearly vegetarian, with fish and very little meat, and was rich in green vegetables and fruits," says Keys. People living on Crete get more than one-third of their calories from fat, most of it from olive oil, which is rich in monounsaturated fatty acids.

Adapted from *www.webmd.org*.

**READING TIP** Dashes (–) can be used to give definitions and examples. For example, the explanation for *primarily vegetarian* (par. 2) is *featuring lots of vegetables, rice and soybeans.*

## Before you read

How much do you know about diets of the world?
Look at these sentences and check (✔) the correct column.

| | Chinese | French | Mediter-ranean | American |
|---|---|---|---|---|
| 1. Lunch is the main meal of the day. | | ✓ | | |
| 2. Most of the fat is in the form of olive oil. | | | | |
| 3. The diet is primarily vegetarian. | | | | |
| 4. Meat is the focus of each meal. | | | | |
| 5. Shavings of meat are used only for flavoring. | | | | |
| 6. The diet is rich in green vegetables and fruit. | | | | |
| 7. The meals are eaten more slowly. | | | | |
| 8. The plate is filled with foods high in saturated fat. | | | | |

## Reading

Scan the text to check your answers. Then read the whole text.

## After you read

**A** What is the tone of the text? Check (✔) the correct answer.

_____ 1. festive            _____ 3. regretful

_____ 2. humorous           _____ 4. thoughtful

**B** Find the words in *italics* in the reading. Then match each word with its meaning. (Be careful! There is one extra answer.)

_h_ 1. *fraction* (par. 1)        a. major

___ 2. *tracking* (par. 3)        b. cause

___ 3. *comprised of* (par. 3)    c. contains

___ 4. *savor* (par. 4)           d. appropriate for

___ 5. *lead to* (par. 4)         e. supported

___ 6. *befitting* (par. 7)       f. having a lot of money

___ 7. *promoted* (par. 7)        g. observing

___ 8. *leading* (par. 7)         h. a small amount

                                  i. slowly enjoy the flavor of

**C** Answer these questions.

1. Which eating habits in the text are similar to yours? Which eating habits should you change to have a healthier diet?
2. How would you describe the typical diet in your country?
3. Think of your favorite meal. Which parts of the meal are healthy? Which are unhealthy?

ing previous owledge

anning

cognizing ne

uessing eaning from ontext

elating ading to ersonal xperience

# Drink, blink, and rest

1 Eyesight is coming under strain as computer work, television viewing, night driving, and even sunshine are making exceptional demands on our eyes. Sunlight, especially in summer, is now regarded as one cause of cataracts.

2 "The thinning of the ozone layer means more short-wave ultraviolet rays are reaching the earth, and these are the biggest risk factor for clouding the lens of the eye," says Jan Bergmanson, a Swedish optometrist.

3 Ultraviolet (UV) rays increase the risk of changes to the cornea – the outer shell of the eyeball – causing clouded vision and eventually cataracts, and can be shielded only by anti-UV lenses. Many fashion sunglasses do not provide sufficient protection.

4 "Poor night vision and eye fatigue are noticeably more common and there has been a big increase in minor eye complaints in the over-40s," says optometrist Dr. Mireille Bonnet, who took part in recent research. She says that the six muscles controlling each eye move more than 100,000 times a day, and that everyone should learn to exercise eye muscles and allow them to rest.

5 It was traditionally thought that near- or far-sightedness were inherited conditions and could not be influenced by environmental factors, but new research is challenging this assumption.

6 Recent research suggests that up to 80 percent of schoolchildren in the United States and western Europe are nearsighted. Years of focusing on close, two-dimensional work causes most children to become at least slightly nearsighted by the age of ten, say the researchers.

7 Problems with night vision, which affect around 25 percent of people, are also on the increase. Using computer screens means the eye operates in electro-magnetic fields that make it work harder, and infra-red from the screen adds to the strain. It is estimated that 25 to 30 percent of people have eye conditions resulting from staring at a screen.

8 Concentrated visual work also slows down the rate of blinking, the process that washes the eyeball with tears and keeps it lubricated. At least 15 percent of people now suffer habitually from dry eyes, says Dr. Bonnet. Office workers are vulnerable because central heating and air conditioning dehydrate the tissues further, as does smoking. Keeping the eye moist has psychological benefits, as dry eyes can make you feel tired.

9 There are two simple remedies to eyestrain: Drink more and blink more. Juan Duran, head of ophthalmology at Cruces Hospital in Bilbao, Spain, recommends closing the eyes for a minute every hour to rest them and retain their humidity. "An increasing number of people come to me with what they call tired eyes or eyestrain, and they sometimes complain of allergies. But the cause is very often dry eyes." Dryness also makes the eyes more susceptible to infection.

10 How to help your eyes:

- When doing close-up work, lift the eyes occasionally to focus on objects in the distance.

- When working on a computer, have a three-dimensional object on top and rest your eyes on it regularly.

- Close your eyes and rest them in the palms of your hands every hour or so.

- Do not stare at a screen or book: blink more.

- Relax! Stress and fatigue have an immediate effect on eyesight, especially in drying the eyes.

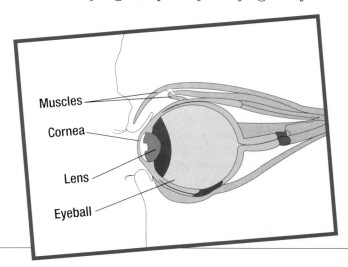

Muscles
Cornea
Lens
Eyeball

Adapted from *The European Magazine.*

## Before you read

**How much do you know about eyesight? Mark each statement true (*T*) or false (*F*).**

   *T*    1. The sun can cause vision problems.

       2. Near- and farsightedness are conditions you can inherit from your parents.

       3. It is important to exercise your eye muscles.

       4. Constantly looking at computer screens can cause sore eyes.

       5. Central heating and air conditioning make your eyes dry.


## Reading

**Scan the text to check your answers. Then read the whole text.**


## After you read

**A**   **Check (✔) the three main ideas in the text.**

       1. the effects of sunlight

       2. eye problems that are increasing

       3. reasons for more eye problems

       4. problems of office workers

       5. fashion sunglasses

       6. best treatment for sore eyes

       7. eye problems in children

       8. the effects of computers


**B**   **Match each word with a word that is similar in meaning.**

   *c*    1. *tired* (par. 8)          a. *regarded* (par. 1)

       2. *protection* (par. 3)       b. *shielded* (par. 3)

       3. *thought* (par. 5)         c. *fatigue* (par. 4)

       4. *work* (par. 7)            d. *operates* (par. 7)

       5. *keeps* (par. 8)           e. *moist* (par. 8)

       6. *lubricated* (par. 8)      f. *retain* (par. 9)

       7. *vulnerable* (par. 8)     g. *susceptible* (par. 9)


**C**   **Answer these questions.**

1. Have you experienced any of the problems described in the text?
   If so, what did you do?
2. Which advice in the text is the most helpful? Which is the least helpful?
3. If you had problems with your eyes, would you give up any activities? If so, which ones?

# Azeri hills hold **secret** of long life

1 You can see for kilometers from the mountains where Allahverdi Ibadov herds his small flock of sheep amid a sea of yellow, red, and purple wildflowers. The view from Amburdere in southern Azerbaijan towards the Iranian border is spectacular, but Mr. Ibadov barely gives it a second glance.

2 Why should he? He's been coming here nearly every day for 100 years.

3 According to his carefully preserved passport, Mr. Ibadov, whose birth was not registered until he was a toddler, is at least 105 years old. His wife, who died two years ago, was even older. They are among the dozens of people in this beautiful, isolated region who live extraordinarily long lives.

4 Mr. Ibadov's eldest son has just turned 70. He lost count long ago of how many grandchildren he has. "I'm an old man now. I look after the sheep and I prepare the wood for winter. I still have something to do."

5 A lifetime of toil, it seems, takes very few people to an early grave in this region. Scientists admit there appears to be something in the Azeri mountains that gives local people a longer, healthier life than most.

6 Miri Ismailov's family in the tiny village of Tatoni are convinced that they know what it is. Mr. Ismailov is 110, his great-great-grandson is four. They share one proud boast: Neither has been to a doctor. "There are hundreds of herbs on the mountain, and we used them all in our cooking and for medicines," explained Mr. Ismailov's daughter, Elmira. "We know exactly what they can do. We are our own doctors."

7 There is one herb for high blood pressure, another for kidney stones, and a third for a hacking cough. They are carefully collected from the slopes surrounding the village. Experts from the Azerbaijan Academy of Science believe the herbs may be part of the answer. They have been studying longevity in this region for years. It began as a rare joint Soviet-American project in the 1980s, but most of the funds have long since dried up.

8 Azeri scientists have isolated a type of saffron unique to the southern mountains as one thing that seems to increase longevity. Another plant, made into a paste, dramatically increases the amount of milk that animals are able to produce. "Now we have to examine these plants clinically to find out which substances have this effect," said Chingiz Gassimov, a scientist at the academy.

9 The theory that local people have also developed a genetic predisposition to long life has been strengthened by the study of a group of Russian émigrés whose ancestors were exiled to the Caucasus 200 years ago. The Russians' life span is much shorter than that of the indigenous mountain folk – though it is appreciably longer than that of their ancestors left behind in the Russian heartland.

10 "Over the decades I believe local conditions have begun to have a positive effect on the new arrivals," Prof. Gassimov said. "It's been slowly transferred down the generations."

11 But Mr. Ismailov, gripping his stout wooden cane, has been around for too long to get overexcited. "There's no secret," he shrugged dismissively. "I look after the cattle and I eat well. Life goes on."

Adapted from *Guardian Weekly*.

## Before you read

Look at the title on the opposite page. Then check (✔) why you think these villagers live such long lives.

_____ 1. hard work      _____ 3. fresh air      _____ 5. sense of humor

_____ 2. good doctors      _____ 4. herbal medicine      _____ 6. healthy diet

## Reading

Scan the text to check your predictions. Then read the whole text.

## After you read

**A** **What do these words refer to?**

1. _it_ (par. 1, line 7)    _the view_      5. _they_ (par. 6, line 2) _____

2. _here_ (par. 2, line 1) _____     6. _They_ (par. 6, line 4) _____

3. _They_ (par. 3, line 5) _____     7. _They_ (par. 7, line 3) _____

4. _he_ (par. 4, line 3) _____     8. _that_ (par. 9, line 6) _____

**B** **Find the words in the reading. Then match each word with its meaning.**

_e_   1. _toddler_ (par. 3)       a. death at a young age

_____ 2. _toil_ (par. 5)       b. the sides of a hill or mountain

_____ 3. _early grave_ (par. 5)       c. made to leave one's own country

_____ 4. _slopes_ (par. 7)       d. hard, physical work

_____ 5. _substance_ (par. 8)       e. a very young child

_____ 6. _émigré_ (par. 9)       f. a type of material

_____ 7. _exiled_ (par. 9)       g. someone who leaves his or her country

**C** **Mark each sentence true (_T_) or false (_F_). Then correct the false sentences.**

                 _region in the mountains of_

_F_   1. Amburdere is a ~~city in~~ southern Azerbaijan.

_____ 2. Allahverdi Ibadov does not know exactly how old he is.

_____ 3. Mr. Ibadov can't do any kind of work anymore.

_____ 4. Miri Ismailov has never been to a doctor but his great-great-grandson has.

_____ 5. Elmira Ismailov is a doctor who uses herbs as medicines.

_____ 6. Scientists think people's genes might affect how long they live.

**D** **Answer these questions.**

1. Do you know anybody over 100 years old? How has this person lived so long?
2. Would you like to live to be 105 years old? Why or why not?
3. Do you prefer modern medicine or medicinal herbs? Why?

## Vocabulary expansion

**A** The abbreviations for these words are used in the dictionary entries below. Match the words with their abbreviations.

_____c_____ 1. noun                                a. *v*

_____ 2. verb                                  b. [C]

_____ 3. adjective                             c. *n*

_____ 4. countable noun                        d. [I]

_____ 5. countable and uncountable noun        e. (fig.)

_____ 6. figurative                            f. [C/U]

_____ 7. intransitive                          g. *adj.*

---

**diet** /ˈdɑi·ət/ *n* [C/U] the food and drink usually taken by a person or group • *a healthy diet includes fresh vegetables.* [C] A diet is also the particular food and drink you are limited to when you cannot eat or drink whatever you want to: a low-salt diet • *I'm going on a diet because I've got to lose some weight.* [C] (fig.) *All you get on TV is a steady diet of violence.*

**diet** /ˈdɑi·ət/ *v* [I] to limit the food that you take, esp. in order to lose weight • *He began dieting a month ago and says he has lost ten pounds already.*
**diet** /ˈdɑi·ət/ *adj* [not gradable] (of food or drink) containing much less sugar than usual and often sweetened artificially, or containing less fat than usual • *He began dieting a month ago and says he has lost ten pounds already.*
**dieter** /ˈdɑi·ət·ər/ *n* [C] • *Studies show there may be as many as 30 million American dieters at any one moment.*

---

**B** Use the dictionary entries above to answer the questions.

1. Write definitions for the words in *italics* in the sentences below. Use your own words.
   a. We have salad for the *dieters*.     _people who limit their food and drink to lose weight_
   b. Ellie's always *dieting*.            _____
   c. I never eat *diet* ice cream         _____
   d. I'm *on a diet*.                     _____

2. Check (✔) the correct sentences. Then correct the incorrect sentences.

   __✓__ a. I need to go on a diet.
   
   _____ b. ~~Dieters~~ *Diet* and exercise are important for good health.
   
   _____ c. She has a special diet because she has health problems.
   
   _____ d. They have been dieting it for several weeks.
   
   _____ e. Jesse has been dieting for several weeks.

## Health and you

A *proverb* is a short popular saying that gives advice about life. What advice do these proverbs give?
1. An apple a day keeps the doctor away.
2. Early to bed, early to rise makes a man healthy, wealthy, and wise.
3. An ounce of prevention is worth a pound of cure.

Work in pairs. Make a list of proverbs related to health. Then join another pair and share your proverbs.

# UNIT 3 Talent

**You are going to read three texts about talent. First, answer the questions in the boxes.**

**READING 1**

## A prodigy in mother's eyes

In this excerpt from a novel, the narrator recalls a time she was pushed by her mother to become a prodigy.

1. As a child, how did your parents encourage you in your schoolwork?
2. As a child, what dreams did your parents have for you?
3. How was your relationship with your parents when you were nine?

**READING 2**

## Born to paint

Read this newspaper article to find out what life is like for a child who is also a very talented artist.

1. Are you artistic? If so, at what age did you realize you had talent?
2. What do you know about child prodigies?
3. What do you think the advantages of being a child prodigy are? The disadvantages?

**READING 3**

## The sound of silence

This newspaper article reveals why Dame Julie Andrews, the movie star with the beautiful voice, isn't singing anymore.

1. Which actors also have beautiful singing voices?
2. Which Julie Andrews movie do you think is the most memorable?
3. What problems do you think professional singers face?

## Vocabulary

**Find out the meanings of the words in *italics*. Then complete the sentences with names of people you know.**

1. _____ has *remarkable* athletic talent.
2. _____ is a *gifted* writer.
3. _____ is a musical *genius*.
4. _____ might suffer from *burnout* in the future.
5. _____ was probably a *precocious* child.
6. _____ suffered a career *setback* recently.

# A prodigy in mother's eyes

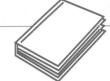

1    Every night after dinner, my mother and I would sit at the Formica® kitchen table. She would present new tests, taking her examples from stories of amazing children she had read in *Ripley's Believe It or Not,* or *Good Housekeeping, Reader's Digest,* and a dozen other magazines she kept in a pile in our bathroom. My mother got these magazines from people whose houses she cleaned. And since she cleaned many houses each week, we had a great assortment. She would look through them all, searching for stories about remarkable children.

2    The first night she brought out a story about a three-year-old boy who knew the capitals of all the states and even most of the European countries. A teacher was quoted as saying the little boy could also pronounce the names of the foreign cities correctly.

3    "What's the capital of Finland?" my mother asked me, looking at the magazine story.

4    All I knew was the capital of California, because Sacramento was the name of the street we lived on in Chinatown. "Nairobi!" I guessed, saying the most foreign word I could think of. She checked to see if that was possibly one way to pronounce "Helsinki" before showing me the answer.

5    The tests got harder – multiplying numbers in my head, finding the queen of hearts in a deck of cards, trying to stand on my head without using my hands, predicting the daily temperatures in Los Angeles, New York, and London.

6    One night I had to look at a page from the Bible for three minutes and then report everything I could remember. "Now Jehoshaphat had riches and honor in abundance and . . . that's all I remember, Ma," I said.

7    And after seeing my mother's disappointed face once again, something inside of me began to die. I hated the tests, the raised hopes and failed expectations. Before going to bed that night, I looked in the mirror above the bathroom sink and when I saw only my face staring back – and that it would always be this ordinary face – I began to cry. Such a sad, ugly girl! I made high-pitched noises like a crazed animal, trying to scratch out the face in the mirror.

8    And then I saw what seemed to be the prodigy side of me – because I have never seen that face before. I looked at my reflection, blinking so I could see more clearly. The girl staring back at me was angry, powerful. This girl and I were the same. I had new thoughts, willful thoughts, or rather thoughts filled with lots of won'ts. I won't let her change me, I promised myself. I won't be what I'm not.

9    So now on nights when my mother presented her tests, I performed listlessly, my head propped on one arm. I pretended to be bored. And I was. I got so bored I started counting the bellows of the foghorns out on the bay while my mother drilled me in other areas. The sound was comforting and reminded me of the cow jumping over the moon. And the next day, I played a game with myself, seeing if my mother would give up on me before eight bellows. After a while I usually counted only one, maybe two bellows at most. At last she was beginning to give up hope.

From *The Joy Luck Club.*

## Before you read

**Check (✔) the things you were tested on when you were a child.**

_____ 1. naming the capitals of foreign countries

_____ 2. multiplying numbers in your head

_____ 3. finding a specific card in a deck of cards

_____ 4. standing on your head without using your hands

_____ 5. predicting daily temperatures in different cities

_____ 6. memorizing poetry and plays

## Reading

**Scan the text to find out which skills the narrator was tested on when she was a child. Then read the whole text.**

## After you read

**A** **The text is from a book. What do you think it is about? Check (✔) the correct answer.**

_____ 1. the secrets of an old woman who thinks she is dying

_____ 2. relationships between Chinese mothers and their American-born daughters

_____ 3. an unhappy childhood during a time of war and poverty

**B** **Find the words in _italics_ in the reading. Then match each word with its meaning.**

_e_ 1. _scratch out_ (par. 7)    a. loud, deep sounds

_____ 2. _willful_ (par. 8)    b. supported

_____ 3. _listlessly_ (par. 9)    c. without energy or interest

_____ 4. _propped_ (par. 9)    d. determined; stubborn

_____ 5. _bellows_ (par. 9)    e. destroy

**C** **Check (✔) the statements that are true.**

_____ 1. The narrator's mother spoke English well.

_____ 2. Sacramento is the capital of California.

_____ 3. The narrator felt bad because her mother was disappointed in her.

_____ 4. The narrator's mother realized her daughter wasn't going to be a prodigy.

_____ 5. The narrator always did her best on her mother's tests.

**D** **Answer these questions.**

1. Do you think the narrator's behavior towards her mother was appropriate? Was the mother right in pressuring her daughter? Why or why not?

2. What were you good at when you were a child? Are you still able to do it?

3. Should parents encourage their children to develop talents? Why or why not?

# Born to paint

1 Ten-year-old Alexandra Nechita has just touched a Picasso at the Museum of Modern Art! Thank goodness nobody has noticed the child prodigy, who's shaking up the art world with her paintings that sell for more than $50,000.

2 An awe-struck Alexandra – "Omigosh, omigosh, look, it's *Three Musicians!*" – met Picasso for the first time at the museum. Her cubist style of painting is often compared with his; some suggest she mimics him. Alexandra simply likes colors. She always has.

3 The youngster has had limited formal instruction but instead graduated naturally from crayons to oils and acrylics. Money was tight for her lab technician parents. In order to afford supplies, they created an exhibit of her works at a local library.

4 To Alexandra, it's all so very simple. "Every child has a talent or a gift," she says. Anyone can be a prodigy "if they wanted to. . . . They can be the biggest of whatever they want to be. It takes dedication, determination, and perseverance. That's it."

5 "That's a typical response from a child prodigy," says Ellen Winner, author of *Gifted Children: Myths and Realities*. "It comes so easily to them that they don't understand why it doesn't come easily to others." Gifted children have what Winner calls "a rage to master."

6 Alexandra's mother, Viorica, is well aware of that "rage." As a toddler, Alexandra spent every waking hour with her coloring books. Fearing their daughter would become introverted, her parents tried to redirect her by taking away the books. Alexandra drew her own shapes to color in. By the time Alexandra was seven, Niki and Viorica Nechita had given in to their child's rage and built a studio in their home.

7 After school and chores, Alexandra paints three to four hours a day. On weekends, she paints all day. She "is typical of someone who has a unitary gift," Winner says. The artist is not precocious in areas outside her artwork. "There's no reason to think she's scholastically gifted or musically gifted."

8 Alexandra calls herself "100 percent normal." Little has changed since the general population discovered her, she says. "There are bigger people that I've met. More media. More exhibits." A book collection of her paintings, *Outside the Lines*, includes personal vignettes written by Alexandra. She's been invited to the White House, and there are other gallery shows planned.

9 Her first painting sold for $50. Today she gets as much as $80,000. To date, Alexandra has sold more than $3 million in paintings.

10 But Winner has concerns about Alexandra's high profile. "These children have enough trouble," she says. There is a "fragile" connection between an early gift and adulthood, and several paths prodigies generally follow. Becoming the "next creative genius" is the most rare outcome, Winner says. Finding success in a similar field is more likely. Burnout is a real threat. But the only thing draining Alexandra right now is the attention. "Thirty interviews in one day," she sighs. Some days she doesn't paint at all. "I understand that I have to be away from it," she says in suddenly grown-up tones. Fame has its price, of course. But "there's nothing I don't like about it."

> **READING TIP** Quotation marks are used to report a speaker's exact words. They may also show that a word has a special meaning in a context that is a little different from the meaning in the dictionary. For example, *a rage to master* (par. 5) means "a strong need to become the best at something."

Adapted from *USA Today*.

## Before you read

Look at the title and the picture on the opposite page. Then check (✔) the information you think you will read about in the text.

_____ 1. Her parents noticed her artistic talent when she was a toddler.

_____ 2. Her first interest in art was with coloring books.

_____ 3. She has had limited formal instruction in art.

_____ 4. She is gifted in music as well as in art.

_____ 5. Her paintings appear in exhibits.

_____ 6. A book of her paintings has been published.

## Reading

Scan the text to check your predictions. Then read the whole text.

## After you read

**A** Find the words in *italics* in the reading. Circle the meaning of each word.

1. When you are *awe-struck*, you feel (fascinated) / **bored** / **depressed**. (par. 2)
2. If you *give in to* something, you **fight against** / **continue to do** / **surrender to** it. (par. 6)
3. If you are *precocious*, you **lack motivation** / **display early talent** / **fear new things**. (par. 7)
4. When you have a *high profile*, people **ignore** / **notice** / **worry** about you. (par. 10)
5. If something *drains* you, it **uses your energy** / **gives you energy** / **makes you happy**. (par. 10)

**B** Cross out the answers that are *not* true.

1. What do child prodigies have in common?
   a. They make a lot of money.
   b. They think it's easy to be a prodigy.
   c. They want to work at what they're good at.
2. How do Alexandra's parents feel about her artistic gift?
   a. They understand she has a gift.
   b. They have stopped worrying she is spending too much time on artwork.
   c. They want her to stop painting.
3. What could Alexandra do in the future that would surprise Ellen Winner?
   a. stop painting completely
   b. open an art gallery
   c. become as famous as Picasso

**C** Answer these questions.

1. If you could have one special talent, what would it be? Why?
2. Do you think that child prodigies have happy lives?
3. What do you think prodigies are like as adults?

edicting

anning

essing
eaning from
ntext

aking
ferences

elating
ading to
ersonal
xperience

# The sound of silence

1 Dame Julie Andrews is the first to admit the past two years have been tough. While the stage version of *The Sound of Music*, the movie that made her a household name, takes Melbourne by storm, Andrews' singing career is on hold – perhaps permanently.

2 As she returns to the public eye to promote her first film in eight years, Andrews still sees herself as a singer first, an actor second. This makes the past couple of years even more traumatic. After she had throat surgery to remove non-cancerous polyps from her vocal cords, the world learned that Andrews may never be able to sing again.

3 Last year, Andrews and her lawyers battled several publications over false gossip when she disappeared from public view. The truth is she had undergone grief therapy to try to cope with her lost voice.

4 And now Andrews' lawyers are busy again, this time with a massive suit against New York's Mount Sinai Hospital and two of its doctors. The lawsuit alleges she was not warned of the possibility of harm to her voice. She is seeking "substantial damages to compensate for loss of past and future earnings."

5 Although there are certain things that Andrews is unable to talk about, pending the lawsuit, she wants to explain what happened. "Somehow the operation went wrong," she says. "It shouldn't have. It was a matter of time, I was told. So I waited patiently. And waited. It's affected the middle register singing voice. My speaking voice has come back, but I still can't yet sing a song."

6 In January she was made a Dame in recognition of her career, as well as her generous charity work. But the question on everyone's lips is: Will the woman who is synonymous with *The Sound of Music* ever sing again? "The stock answer, when anyone asks that question, is absolutely genuine," Andrews says. "I'm still very optimistic. I have to be. I can't think of the alternative. But it's very definitely a major setback. I am either supremely optimistic or in denial."

7 "I think to some degree, I'm in a form of denial about it because to not sing with an orchestra, to not be able to communicate through my voice, which I've done all my life, and not to be able to phrase lyrics and give people that kind of joy, I think I would be totally devastated."

8 The public learned of the outcome of the operation when her husband told a magazine: "If you heard (her voice), you'd weep . . . I don't think she'll sing again. It's an absolute tragedy." "That just about sums it up," Andrews says. "Yes, it is a tragedy. Thankfully, I wasn't younger. But I mean, at least I've had a wonderful career . . . I'm still hoping that it will reverse itself. But it's been a long time now. My doctors don't hold out much hope, but say that I should continue practicing."

9 "I don't feel ready to retire . . . I seem to be as busy as ever, though maybe one isn't doing as much as one used to. Still, it doesn't stop the joy of doing it when you do it."

Adapted from *Herald Sun*.

dicting

nning

essing
aning from
text

derstanding
in ideas

elating
ading to
ersonal
xperience

## Before you read

**Read the first paragraph on the opposite page. Then answer the following question.**

Why do you think Andrews' singing career was on hold at the time this article was written?

## Reading

**Scan the text to check your prediction. Then read the whole text.**

## After you read

**A** **Find the words in *italics* in the reading. Then match each word with its meaning.**

    _c_    1. *traumatic* (par. 2)      a. suffering emotional distress or pain

          2. *undergone* (par. 3)      b. money paid for causing injury or loss

          3. *suit* (par. 4)      c. shocking and upsetting

          4. *alleges* (par. 4)      d. experienced

          5. *damages* (par. 4)      e. pay money for something lost or damaged

          6. *compensate* (par. 4)      f. a legal problem taken to court

          7. *denial* (par. 7)      g. states that something is a fact

          8. *devastated* (par. 7)      h. refusal to believe something

**B** **The writer asked Julie Andrews these questions. Write the number of the paragraph or paragraphs next to the question it answers. Write *X* if the question is not answered in the text.**

    _X_    a. When did you first start singing?

          b. Why did you have surgery?

          c. What kind of help has your husband given you?

          d. Will you ever sing again?

          e. Are you looking forward to your retirement?

          f. Do you think you're in denial about the future?

          g. Why are you in a legal fight with doctors?

**C** **Answer these questions.**

1. Do you think Julie Andrews should receive money for her loss? If so, how much should she get?
2. Is it worse to lack talent or to have talent and then to lose it completely? Why?
3. How much do you know about your favorite singers' careers? When did they start singing? What difficulties did they face?

## Vocabulary expansion

**A** Find the phrasal verbs below in this unit's readings. Then write the letter of the correct definition next to each phrasal verb. (Be careful! There are two extra definitions.)

_d_  1. *give up on* (reading 1, par. 9)

_____  2. *give up hope* (reading 1, par. 9)

_____  3. *shaking up* (reading 2, par. 1)

_____  4. *taking away* (reading 2, par. 6)

_____  5. *given in to* (reading 2, par. 6)

_____  6. *has come back* (reading 3, par. 5)

_____  7. *sums . . . up* (reading 3, par. 8)

_____  8. *hold out . . . hope* (reading 3, par. 8)

a. removing
b. continue to move or travel
c. continue to expect something good
d. stop waiting for someone to do something
e. has returned

f. briefly says the most important facts
g. has left
h. stop wishing for something
i. making big changes in something
j. agreed to after much debate

**B** Answer the questions.

1. If your friends always wanted to stay home and watch TV, would you give up on them or try to convince them to go out?
2. Would it be easy for you to give up chocolate? What about coffee? Ice cream? Soda?
3. Did your parents ever give in to something you wanted? If so, what was it?
4. How would you sum up your reading skills?
5. Have you ever lost the ability to do something? Did it ever come back to you?
6. Who is shaking up the music world these days?
7. Have you ever wanted a special talent? Do you hold out hope that you will achieve it?

## Talent and you

Work in small groups. Imagine that your class is going to have a talent show. Discuss what talents you have and what you can contribute to the talent show. (Be imaginative: Some people can play a musical instrument, but others may be able to cook well or tell funny stories.) Then share your ideas with your classmates.

# 4 Beauty

**You are going to read three texts about beauty. First, answer the questions in the boxes.**

**READING 1**

## Executives go under the knife

Do you want to know the secret to success? Discover how cosmetic surgery is helping people get ahead in the workplace.

1. Do you know anyone who has had cosmetic surgery? Why did they undergo the surgery?
2. How important is appearance for success in business?
3. Is appearance equally important for male and female executives?

**READING 2**

## What makes a man attractive?

What features make a man handsome? Read this newspaper article to learn the surprising results of a recent study.

1. What do you think makes someone beautiful?
2. Do you think different cultures have the same ideas about beauty?
3. How important is beauty in choosing a mate?

**READING 3**

## In the land of the mirror

This magazine article takes a look at one country where winning beauty pageants is serious business.

1. Do you like to watch beauty pageants? Why or why not?
2. Are televised beauty pageants popular shows in your country?
3. Why do you think some women compete in beauty pageants?

## Vocabulary

**Find out the meanings of the words in *italics*. Then check (✔) the answers you think are true.**

| | Men | Women |
|---|---|---|
| 1. Who must have more *appeal* to succeed in business? | | |
| 2. Who must be more *attractive* to appear on TV? | | |
| 3. Who pays more attention to the world of *glamor*? | | |
| 4. Who is more interested in marrying a *knockout*? | | |
| 5. Who pays attention to their *looks*? | | |
| 6. Who is more *vain*? | | |

# Executives go under the knife

1   A growing number of executives are investing in plastic surgery to get ahead in the workplace, a new study has revealed.

2   Spending on cosmetic surgery in the UK has risen by more than a third – driven by the rising number of businessmen and women who are going under the knife to help them climb the career ladder.

3   The trend reflects frustration among a growing number of female executives who feel that a better physical appearance may finally help them break through the glass ceiling in male-dominated companies.

4   Other business people of both sexes fear that they may be replaced by younger, better-looking colleagues, or be passed over for promotion because their employers think they look tired or old.

5   A report by Mintel, a market analysis firm, says: "A work culture which often equates youth with energy and ambition, and maturity with irrelevance and lack of innovation, has encouraged the use of cosmetic surgery by men and women to reduce signs of aging and so improve their job prospects."

6   The report also points out that while plastic surgery is traditionally considered the preserve of women, male executives are starting to catch on to its perceived advantages.

7   Mintel says people in the UK will spend an estimated 150 million pounds on plastic surgery this year – representing about 72,000 operations. Overall, the market has grown by 31 percent in recent years.

**Executive A**

**Executive B**

8   Nearly half of working women questioned said they would consider having cosmetic surgery and nearly a fifth of female managers said they believed it would improve their self-esteem.

9   A recent study showed that among working women, plastic surgery is the third most common reason for asking for a bank loan – behind buying a car or paying for a vacation.

10   Peter Coles, a director of a medical group which runs ten cosmetic surgery clinics, estimated that about 30 percent of working women are having cosmetic surgery for reasons related to their jobs. "There has been an increase in businessmen and businesswomen coming forward for surgery," he said.

11   "These are people that are perhaps a little older than their competitors in the workplace and want to have as young-looking and attractive a face as possible. This is probably of greater concern to men than women."

12   Coles said that women hoping to use cosmetic surgery to get ahead in business tend to have facelifts, face peeling, laser skin resurfacing, and collagen replacement therapy. Men tend to be more worried about the bags under their eyes.

13   According to the Mintel study, the biggest growth in spending has been on sub-surgical procedures, most commonly used to reduce the appearance of facial wrinkles.

14   Despite the rise in work-related cosmetic surgery, Lesley Kidd, a recruitment consultant, said: "Without doubt, looking attractive is helpful in the workplace, but I do believe that someone with better skills and ability will beat someone who only has good looks in an interview nine times out of ten. Your looks might help you feel more confident, but they won't necessarily help you in your job."

**READING TIP**   You don't need to know every word in a text to understand the main idea. For example, you don't need to know the exact meaning of *facelifts, face peeling, laser skin resurfacing,* and *collagen replacement therapy* (par. 12). It is enough to know that they are treatments performed using cosmetic surgery.

Adapted from *The Scotsman.*

ating to
topic
anning
essing
aning from
ntext
nderstanding
etails
Relating
eading to
personal
experience

## Before you read

Look at the pictures on the opposite page. Then complete the sentences with *Executive A, Executive B,* or *Neither executive.*

1. _____ looks more energetic.

2. _____ looks less ambitious.

3. _____ has lower self-esteem.

4. _____ is more likely to get a promotion at work.

## Reading

Scan the text to find out how executives in the United Kingdom would complete these questions. Then read the whole text.

## After you read

**A** **Find the words and phrases in the reading that match these definitions. Write one word on each line.**

1. having an operation          *going   under   the   knife* (par. 2)

2. be successful at work          ____ ____ ____ ____ (par. 2)

3. a point beyond which some people          ____ ____ (par. 3)
   usually aren't promoted

4. not chosen          ____ ____ (par. 4)

5. opportunities          ____ (par. 5)

6. something only one group does          ____ (par. 6)

7. loose skin under eyes          ____ (par. 12)

**B** **Complete each sentence with *men, women,* or *men and women.***

1. More *men and women* are undergoing cosmetic surgery than in the past.

2. _____ think looking tired or old will cause them to lose their jobs.

3. Almost 50 percent of working _____ might have cosmetic surgery.

4. Almost 20 percent of _____ in management positions said cosmetic surgery would help them feel good about themselves.

5. _____ are especially worried about younger-looking employees who have the same positions as they do.

6. The biggest worry for _____ is bags under the eyes.

**C** **Answer these questions.**

1. Would you consider having cosmetic surgery to help your career?
2. For which types of work is appearance most important?
3. How would you feel if a younger or better-looking colleague got a promotion you deserved?

# What makes a man attractive?

1  You know it instinctively when you see it walking toward you, or on a giant movie screen. A beautiful woman. A handsome man. Throughout the ages, a woman with delicate features, high cheekbones, full lips, and large, wide eyes has been considered a great beauty. For a man, the assumption has been that the more rugged, the thicker the eyebrows, thinner the lips and deep-set the eyes, the more attractive. Right?

2  According to new and controversial research, not exactly. In a study published in the journal *Nature*, Scottish researchers report that both the men and women they studied found a slightly feminized male face more attractive. Consider the mysterious appeal of actor Leonardo DiCaprio.

3  The scientists found the preference appeared to hold true across three cultures surveyed: 92 men and women in Japan, South Africa, and Scotland picked more feminine male faces as the most handsome. "The finding came as a real surprise to us," said David Perrett, a psychologist and one of the study's authors. "Individuals may differ in their preferences, but if you look at what the majority like, they chose the slightly feminized male face." The more masculine the face, the more the people studied associated it with coldness, dishonesty, and dominance. The feminized male face was seen as emotionally warm, someone who would be a faithful husband and a cooperative, loving father.

4  Not everyone in the growing field of "beauty research" agrees with the findings, although they agree the perception of beauty is a powerful influence on behavior. According to Perrett

**Leonardo DiCaprio**

and his colleagues, it has everything to do with how people choose their mates.

5  Under this theory, humans seek to preserve the species by producing the next generation. To ensure success, men tend to choose young women with delicate facial features who appear more likely to bear healthy children.

6  Women's choices are a bit more complicated. Previous studies show that some clearly have preferred big, muscular men. As cavemen hunters, they could provide the best food. Their physical strength meant their immune systems were robust and their genes good for producing healthy children. These men usually had protruding foreheads, heavy eyebrows, thin lips, small, deep-set eyes, and large noses and jaws. Think Arnold Schwarzenegger.

7  However, Perrett and his colleagues refer to other studies showing this type of man was more likely to exhibit aggressive behavior. Thus, Perrett argues, women might be choosing those whose faces give the appearance they'll be more likely to help raise the children.

**Arnold Schwarzenegger**

8  Perrett's conclusions are already provoking debate. "If women find slightly less testosterone effects more attractive, why just apply it to the face?" said one anthropologist who reviewed the paper. "Ask women what they're looking for in a mate: Have they ever said shortness rather than tallness? Do they want shoulders a little narrower than average? I don't think so."

9  "From everything we know from science, from everyday experience, and from other animal species about what makes a man attractive, I would not rush to conclude that women really like slightly feminine, nurturing daddies for mates."

Adapted from *The Gazette*.

## Before you read

king about
sonal
erience

**What features do you think women find attractive in men? Check the items.**

_____ 1. high cheekbones      _____ 6. deep-set eyes

_____ 2. rugged looks      _____ 7. wide eyes

_____ 3. heavy eyebrows      _____ 8. a large jaw

_____ 4. full lips      _____ 9. a protruding forehead

_____ 5. delicate features      _____ 10. a slightly feminized face

## Reading

nning

**Scan the text to see how women answered this question in studies. Then read the whole text.**

## After you read

lerstanding
erence
rds

**A** **What do these words refer to?**

1. *it* (par. 1, line 1)    *beauty*    4. *those* (par. 7, line 6) _____

2. *it* (par. 3, line 16) _____    5. *they* (par. 7, line 8) _____

3. *it* (par. 4, line 7) _____    6. *they* (par. 8, line 7) _____

lerstanding
t
anization

**B** **Write the number of the paragraph or paragraphs next to each subject. (Be careful! There are two extra subjects.)**

a. _2, 3_ conclusions from Perrett's study

b. _____ reasons attractive men and women succeed

c. _____ arguments against Perrett's study

d. _____ common assumptions about beauty

e. _____ studies that agree with Perrett's study

f. _____ how perception of beauty affects human behavior

derstanding
:ails

**C** **Find and correct the ten mistakes in the summary of the study. (Note! The first mistake has been corrected.)**

                   *Scotland*

Researchers in ~~Japan~~ interviewed men and women in two countries. They found that men prefer feminine male faces, but women prefer masculine male faces. Psychologist David Perrett is not surprised about the findings. He says people associate masculine faces with emotional warmth, faithfulness, and cooperation; however, they associate feminine faces with coldness, dishonesty, and dominance. According to Perrett, years ago men chose women who seemed likely to provide good food, while women chose men for less complicated reasons. The study was published in a textbook called *Nature*.

lating
ading to
rsonal
perience

**D** **Answer these questions.**

1. Do you agree with Perrett's findings? What examples can you give?

2. What actors do you think are good-looking? Can you describe their facial features?

3. Think of men you know who have masculine faces. What are their characters like?

# In the land of the mirror

1 In much of Latin America, soccer is the popular passion, but here it is beauty pageants. Everyone, it seems, knows the Miss Venezuela anthem, and the final in September is the top-rated TV show. Though a nation of just 24 million, Venezuela is a beauty-pageant superpower.

2 In the past 25 years, it has won the crown eight times in the top two contests, Miss Universe and Miss World, which is more than any other country. Locals credit their melting pot of backgrounds – European, African, and Indian – with producing one knockout after another. But the real reason has more to do with applying industrial-type efficiency to turning out beauty queens.

3 The undisputed captain of that industry is Osmel Sousa, for 25 years head of the Miss Venezuela Organization. He and his scouts comb malls, universities, and beaches for the "rough diamonds" who will be cut and polished to near perfection – by his definition, anyway. Sousa has help from 25 specialists: plastic surgeons, dentists, dermatologists, dietitians, hair and makeup experts, personal trainers, and psychologists. He looks at women the way a sculptor views a piece of clay: "I mold the person," he says proudly. "I derive my enjoyment by changing the women for the better. Otherwise, it would be a bore."

4 Skin too light or too dark? Creams can handle that. Gummy smile or biggish nose? Surgery can remake it. Appraisals can be harsh. "Oh my God, she has too much chin and her lips are too big!" gasps dermatologist Sonia Roffe, as one contestant struts by. "We'd have to fix that."

5 The wannabe Misses regard Sousa's glamour factory as a ticket to the good life. "This organization can launch my career," says Ilana Furman, 20, who has wanted to be a Miss since she was seven. "It's the dream of all Venezuelan girls." Still, she has some anxiety. "Osmel said I have a thick nose," she frets. "I told the organization I don't want them to touch my face. . . . I hope they can fix it with cosmetics."

6 Workouts. The fitness and food regimen is tough. Margie Rosales, 19, a college communications major, was a winner in the Caracas casting but admits that daily six-hour gym workouts and a menu of chicken breasts, egg whites, and seaweed can get her down. "I was depressed because the diet was really hard," she says. "I've put a lot into this."

7 Other Venezuelans put a lot into looks, too. This nation leads Latin America in per capita spending on cosmetics. A Roper Starch Worldwide poll of 30 countries last year found that Venezuelans are the vainest of them all: Sixty-five percent of women and 47 percent of men said they think about their looks "all the time."

8 Here in Beauty Land, schools and clubs pick beauty queens from an early age. Doting fathers give their daughters a nose job for their 16th birthday. Astrid Cabral, 18, an accounting student visiting a hair salon, says she plans to have her breasts enlarged to heed her boyfriend's call to "be like a Miss." Says Cabral: "It's more important to be smart, but the sad fact is that women in Venezuela are forced to concentrate on their own beauty because men demand it."

From *US News & World Report.*

## Before you read

The article on the opposite page was written by a journalist in Venezuela.
Check (✔) the information you think you will read about in the text.

_____ 1. Venezuela has won more international beauty pageants than any other country.

_____ 2. It costs a lot of money to enter beauty pageants.

_____ 3. Experts change women in order to win beauty pageants.

_____ 4. Contestants get help from dermatologists, dietitians, and plastic surgeons.

_____ 5. Many Venezuelans criticize their country's interest in beauty pageants.

_____ 6. Venezuela leads Latin America in spending on cosmetics.


## Reading

Scan the text to check your predictions. Then read the whole text.


## After you read

**A** Find the words in *italics* in the reading. Then match each word with its meaning. (Be careful! There are two extra answers.)

| | | |
|---|---|---|
| _a_ | 1. *appraisals* (par. 4) | a. judgments |
| _____ | 2. *harsh* (par. 4) | b. causing someone to lose |
| _____ | 3. *gasps* (par. 4) | c. cruel |
| _____ | 4. *struts* (par. 4) | d. showing a lot of love |
| _____ | 5. *launch* (par. 5) | e. walks in a proud way |
| _____ | 6. *doting* (par. 8) | f. wanting to be beautiful |
| | | g. help begin |
| | | h. says while taking in a short quick breath |

**B** Check (✔) the writer's main purpose in writing the text.

_____ 1. to inform

_____ 2. to inspire

_____ 3. to entertain

**C** Answer these questions.

1. Do you think about your looks a lot, a little, or not at all?
2. Would you like to have someone like Osmel Sousa help improve your appearance? Why or why not?
3. What would you advise a young girl who showed an interest in beauty pageants?

## Vocabulary expansion

**A** Write the words under the correct headings. Then add your own words to the chart.

attractive    elegant        handsome    rugged
beautiful     good-looking   lovely      striking
cute          gorgeous       pretty      stunning

| Referring only to men | Referring only to women | Referring to men and women |
|---|---|---|
| | | attractive |
| | | |
| | | |
| | | |
| | | |
| | | |

**B** Complete each sentence with the name of a famous person. Then compare your sentences with another student.

1. _____ is attractive.

2. _____ is beautiful.

3. _____ is cute.

4. _____ is elegant.

5. _____ is good-looking.

6. _____ is gorgeous.

7. _____ is handsome.

8. _____ is lovely.

9. _____ is pretty.

10. _____ is rugged.

11. _____ is striking.

12. _____ is stunning.

## Beauty and you

Bring in a picture of someone you consider handsome or beautiful. Tell the class why you think the person is handsome or beautiful. Find out whether others agree with you.

# UNIT 5 Technology

**You are going to read three texts about technology. First, answer the questions in the boxes.**

**READING 1**

## The car that thinks it's your friend

Read this newspaper article to learn about a futuristic car that might be the perfect vehicle for you.

1. Do you drive? If so, what do you like about the car you drive? What do you dislike?
2. What is the most important thing to consider when buying a car?
3. What features do you think cars of the future will have?

**READING 2**

## Information, please!

This excerpt from a website looks at the latest technology to verify people's identity.

1. How often do you use a password or PIN (personal identification number) to prove your identity?
2. What problems have you had with passwords or PINs?
3  What is the best way to verify someone's identity?

**READING 3**

## Researchers worry as teens grow up online

This newspaper article describes some problems that result from teenagers spending a lot of time online.

1. What hobbies are good for teenagers? Which could be harmful?
2. Where do teens hang out in your city or town?
3. Is spending time on the Internet good for teens? Why or why not?

## Vocabulary

**Find out the meanings of the words in *italics*. Then answer the questions.**

1. How many *keystrokes* can you type per minute on the computer?
2. Have you ever *downloaded* computer *software*?
3. Have you ever *scanned* photos onto a computer disk?
4. How much time do you spend in *cyberspace*?
5. Do you ever play computer games with a *joystick*?

# The car that thinks it's your friend

1   The touchy-feely car of the future is so sensitive that it can be driven to tears.

2   Crying headlights, a grinning hood, and a wagging tail that protrudes from the trunk are among the mood-emulating features of Pod, a new concept vehicle that was unveiled by Toyota and Sony at the Tokyo motor show.

3   The car is intended as a four-wheeled friend. While the comfort offered by other cars stops at plush seats and air conditioning, Pod aims to provide affection, sympathy, and encouragement. Like a dog welcoming its master, the car sits up, wags its tail, and acknowledges its owner's presence using hydraulics and a multi-colored light-emitting diode (LED) display panel across the front.

4   While on the road, the car constantly monitors the driver's mood with pulse and sweat sensors on the joystick. (There is no wheel.) Cameras focused on the eyes keep watch for any sign of drowsiness. If a driver appears to be losing his or her cool, Pod will display warnings, play soothing music, and blow cold air at the face. Sleepy drivers are shaken awake with loud music and a vibrating chair.

5   To improve driving skills, Pod compares acceleration, braking, and steering with the optimum performance recorded by professionals. It uses this comparison to score drivers, offer advice, and rank all Pod owners.

6   Toyota claims that the car will eventually be able to learn its owner's likes and dislikes by monitoring passenger conversations. If the car hears a favorite song being discussed, it will download the track from the Internet and play it without being asked. It will also recommend restaurants that might suit the driver's taste and take photographs of passengers when they sound particularly happy.

7   In keeping with the moodiness that is the car's main selling point, Pod expresses a form of road rage. If a driver brakes or swerves suddenly, the LED panel on the hood glowers a furious red and the tail pricks up at the back.

8   Anger is one of the car's ten "emotional states." Another is sadness – a blue front with tear-shaped lights seemingly dripping from the headlights – which appears after a flat tire or when gas is low.

9   "Most images of cars in the future are menacing, like in *Blade Runner*. We wanted to show that they can be cheerful and entertaining," said Yasunori Sakamoto, part of the Toyota design team.

10   Mr. Sakamoto said Toyota has no plans to put Pod on the market. Sad, really.

> **READING TIP**
> Sometimes a writer expresses humor by using a *pun*, a word or expression that sounds like another word but has a different meaning. For example, the expression *driven to tears* (par.1), meaning "caused to cry," is used to describe a car, which is something you drive.

Adapted from *The Guardian*.

ating to the
ic

anning

essing
aning from
ntext

derstanding
tails

lating
ading to
rsonal
perience

## Before you read

**Check (✔) the features you would like your next car to have.**

_____ 1. an appearance that changes according to your mood

_____ 2. a computer and movie screen for every passenger

_____ 3. an engine that doesn't need gasoline

_____ 4. the ability to give you affection, sympathy, and encouragement

_____ 5. a computer that controls speed, steers, and checks road conditions

## Reading

**Scan the text to find out which features above are in the car of the future. Then read the whole text.**

## After you read

**A** **Find the words in _italics_ in the reading. Write the words or phrases on the line next to the correct heading.**

| | | | |
|---|---|---|---|
| _drowsiness_ (par. 4) | _hood_ (par. 2) | _sits up_ (par. 2) | _wags its tail_ (par. 3) |
| _headlights_ (par. 2) | _lose one's cool_ (par. 4) | _trunk_ (par. 3) | |

1. parts of a car      _hood, trunk_
2. a dog's reactions      _____
3. drivers' reactions      _____

**B** **Check (✔) the statements a Pod owner would _not_ make.**

✓   1. My car doesn't understand me.

_____ 2. My car always looks happy to see me.

_____ 3. My car can tell when I'm nervous or angry.

_____ 4. If I fall asleep, my car will automatically brake.

_____ 5. If I start to fall asleep, my seat will vibrate.

_____ 6. My car lets me know if I'm a good driver.

_____ 7. My car laughs when I tell a joke.

_____ 8. My car played some music that it knew I liked.

**C** **Answer these questions.**

1. Which features of Pod do you like? Which do you dislike? Why?
2. Which car would you most like to own? Why?
3. If you could design the perfect car, what features would it have?

# Identification, please!

1 "Iris Scan please," the bank's computer voice tells you. You step up and the computer reads your eye, comparing it to the stored file it has of your iris. The images had better match – otherwise, you won't be able to get your money.

2 Many science fiction films have used technologies such as iris, fingerprint, or voice scans as part of the story. Well, folks, believe it or not, these seemingly advanced technologies may soon be prevalent at work, the bank, the airport, and your local prison. The iris scan, fingerprint scan, and voice scan are all examples of biometrics, an exploding area of automatic personal identification technology. Basically, biometrics uses various means of identity verification based on an individual's unique physiological and/or behavioral characteristics. These tests generally compare the captured image to a stored image, checking for matches in the particular pattern or characteristic being tested.

3 Biometrics technologies can be used to verify fingerprints, voices, irises, body heat patterns, facial images, handprints, signatures, and even computer keystroke rhythms. To increase accuracy, multiple biometrics verification systems can be employed. Biometrics verification is currently in use in some airports, prisons, and hospitals to help control restricted access areas, and is being used by law enforcement and government agencies as well.

4 Biometrics identification systems have a number of advantages over password or PIN (personal identification number) systems. Primarily, the individual who is to be identified has to be physically present to be identified. Secondarily, there are no passwords to remember, forget, forge, lose, or steal.

5 Biometrics technology has recently become much more accessible, mainly due to the fact that the costs associated with implementing the technology are plummeting. Many companies have begun to adopt biometrics identification systems, which often employ scanners and embedded cameras, to give their large computer networks stronger security than a mere password-only protection system could ever provide.

6 Perhaps the simplest and most affordable form of biometrics is the voice scan. All that is required for a simple voice scan is a computer, microphone, and the correct software (microphones are commonly included with computers). The software records the subject's voice and compares it with a stored voice sample for identification purposes.

7 For added security, finger and handprint scans can also be employed. Fingerprint scans compare a print scan to a stored file, while handprint scans measure a hand's unique geometric aspects.

8 Iris scans currently give the highest level of accuracy among the available biometrics systems. Full facial scans are currently being implemented at border crossings and airports. Facial scanning equipment can actually track and identify moving faces within a crowd.

9 The potential of biometrics is exciting and encouraging. There is little doubt that continued development, testing, and application will improve current technologies. Soon, the days of car keys, passwords, and PINs will be gone. Just don't leave home without your fingerprints!

Adapted from *NetWeek*.

dicting

nning

:ognizing
pose

derstanding
:ails

.lating
ading to
.rsonal
perience

# Before you read

**Look at these phrases from the text about *biometrics technology*. What do you think the term *biometrics technology* means? Write a definition.**

iris scan
voice scan
identity verification
physiological and/or behavioral characteristics

stored image
fingerprint scan
embedded cameras
stored file

biometrics technology: _____

# Reading

**Scan the text to check your prediction. Then read the whole text.**

# After you read

**A** **Check (✔) the writer's main purpose in writing the text.**

_____ 1. to compare biometrics with other identification technologies

_____ 2. to discuss the pros and cons of biometrics technology

_____ 3. to inform people about biometrics technology

_____ 4. to persuade people to invest in biometrics technology

**B** **Mark each sentence true (*T*), false (*F*), or does not give the information (*?*).**

___?___ 1. Some people object to the use of biometrics technology.

_____ 2. Biometrics technology is not in use now.

_____ 3. Biometrics technology is a big industry.

_____ 4. Biometrics technology can measure many different things.

_____ 5. Fingerprint and handprint scans measure the same things.

_____ 6. All biometrics technologies are equally accurate.

_____ 7. Biometrics technology verifies identity more accurately than passwords
and PINs.

_____ 8. There can be problems with biometrics technology.

_____ 9. Biometrics technology uses stored information to verify identity.

**C** **Answer these questions.**

1. Which biometrics identification systems in the article are used in your country?
Where are they used?
2. What are the advantages of biometrics technology? The disadvantages?
3. Are you against using biometrics identification systems in any particular places
(for example, school, work, apartment buildings, banks, hospitals, or airports)?
If so, why?

# Researchers worry as teens grow up online

1   Teens don't understand the big fuss. As the first generation to grow up in a wired world, they hardly know a time when computers weren't around, and they leap at the chance to spend hours online, chatting with friends. So what?

2   But researchers nationwide are increasingly concerned that, as cyberspace replaces the pizza parlor as the local hangout, adolescents are becoming more isolated, less adept at interpersonal relationships, and perhaps numb to the small – and big – deceptions that are so much a part of the e-mail world. Researchers are asking just how the futures of teenagers are changed when so many of them are spending an hour or two on the Internet each day, replacing face-to-face contact with computer contact.

3   "We're not only looking at what the computer can do *for* us, but what are they doing *to* us," said sociologist Sherry Turkle. "It's on so many people's minds." She wants to know how a teen's sense of self and values may be altered in a world where personal connections and the creation of new identities can be limitless.

4   Social psychologist Robert Kraut said he's concerned about the "opportunity costs" of so much online time for youths. He found that teens who used computers, even just a few hours a week, showed increased signs of loneliness and social isolation. In his study of 100 families that use the Internet, Kraut said these teens reported having fewer friends to hang around with, possibly because their computer time replaced hours they would have spent with others. "Chatting online may be better than watching television, but it's worse than hanging out with real friends," he said.

5   Today's teens, however, don't see anything strange in the fact that the computer screen occupies a central place in their social lives. "School is stressful and busy. There's almost no time to just hang out," said Parker Rice, 17. "Talking online is just catch-up time."

6   Many teens acknowledge there's an unreal quality to their cyberspace communication, including their odd shorthand terms, such as POS (parent over shoulder) or LOL (laughing out loud). Psychologists see this code as part of the exclusive shared language that teenagers love.

7   When it comes to e-mail exchanges, teens also show a remarkable tolerance for each other's fudges or deceptions. Nor are they surprised when a mere acquaintance unloads a personal secret through e-mail. Nobody seems to expect the online world to be the same as the real world. Jonathon Reis, 14, didn't seem the least bit put off when he learned that a girl wasn't totally honest when she described herself online. "I know it's likely they'll say they look better than they do," he said.

8   Teens say they also appreciate the ability to edit what they say online, or take the time to think about a response. As cowardly as it may seem, some teens admit that asking someone for a date, or breaking up, can be easier in message form. But they insist there's no harm intended, and cyberspace has become just another medium – like the telephone – in the world of adolescence.

Adapted from *The Boston Globe.*

## Before you read

dicting

Look at the picture on the opposite page. Then check (✔) the information you think you will read about in the text.

_____ 1. problems teens have developing interpersonal relationships

_____ 2. stories about teen violence resulting from online activities

_____ 3. opinions of teens about their online activities

_____ 4. concerns of parents about their teenage children's computer habits

_____ 5. effects of online activities on the health of teens

## Reading

Scan the text to check your predictions. Then read the whole text.

## After you read

**A** Find the words in *italics* in the reading. Then match each word with its meaning.

_c_ 1. *isolated* (par. 2)       a. written with abbreviations and symbols

_____ 2. *adept* (par. 2)        b. talk about a problem

_____ 3. *numb to* (par. 2)      c. separated and alone

_____ 4. *shorthand* (par. 6)    d. not concerned or bothered by

_____ 5. *fudge* (par. 7)        e. skillful

_____ 6. *unload* (par. 7)       f. concerned or bothered

_____ 7. *put off* (par. 7)      g. a dishonest statement

**B** Mark each statement Researcher's opinion (*R*) or Teenager's opinion (*T*).

_R_ 1. Spending a lot of time online affects teenagers' ability to form relationships.

_____ 2. Teens who use computers to chat to spend less time with friends.

_____ 3. There's nothing wrong with teens spending hours online.

_____ 4. Every hour that teens are online is one hour less they could spend with a friend.

_____ 5. The Internet provides a way to keep in touch with friends.

_____ 6. It's all right for people not to be completely honest when they're online.

_____ 7. Communicating online allows more time to think about what to say.

_____ 8. Teens might be developing a different sense of what's right and wrong.

**C** Answer these questions.

1. How much time spent online do you think is too much? Why?
2. Do you think that everything can be communicated by e-mail? Or are some things best said face-to-face? What examples can you give?
3. Would it bother you if people lied to you online about their age or appearance? Why or why not?

## Vocabulary expansion

**A** Match each shorthand term with its meaning. Be careful! There are two extra answers. (Answers appear below.)

_i_ 1. LOL          a. be seeing you

___ 2. cm          b. call me

___ 3. cul8r          c. end of discussion

___ 4. h2cus          d. gotta go

___ 5. idk          e. hope to see you soon

___ 6. wot          f. I don't know

___ 7. j4f          g. I'll look into it

___ 8. g2g          h. just for fun

___ 9. ppl          i. laughing out loud

___ 10. eod          j. people

k. see you later

l. what

**B** Write what you think each shorthand term means. (Answers appear below.)

1. POS          _parent over shoulder_

2. wan2          _____

3. b4          _____

4. ruok          _____

5. 2moro          _____

6. gr8          _____

7. bf / gf          _____

8. 2dA          _____

## Technology and you

Think of five other shorthand terms you could use to chat with someone online. Then ask your classmates to guess what they mean.

ANSWERS: A. 1. i 2. b 3. k 4. e 5. f 6. l 7. h 8. d 9. j 10. c
B. 1. parent over shoulder 2. want to 3. before 4. are you OK 5. tomorrow 6. great 7. boyfriend/girlfriend 8. today

# UNIT 6 Punishment

You are going to read three texts about punishment. First, answer the questions in the boxes.

## Spanking on trial

This magazine article reports on an American who was arrested in Canada for spanking his daughter.

1. Is spanking a common punishment in your country?
2. Have you ever seen a parent strike his or her child?
3. What kinds of laws should protect children from parental punishment? Why?

## The Letter

In this excerpt from a novel, a girl gets into trouble with her mother for receiving a letter.

1. Have you ever angered your parents? If so, how?
2. Have your parents ever disapproved of your friends? If so, why?
3. Have your parents ever made you do something you didn't want to do? If so, what?

## Schools take the fun out of suspension

This newspaper article describes how suspension is changing in some California schools.

1. Do schools in your country suspend students?
2. In your country, is cleaning the school a duty or a punishment?
3. How do you think parents feel when their child is suspended from school?

## Vocabulary
**Find out the meanings of the words in *italics*. Then answer the questions.**

1. Did you often *act up* when you were a child?
2. What kind of punishment should parents *inflict* on their children?
3. If you were a teacher, what would you do if your students were *insolent*?
4. What should be done about students who have a bad *attitude*?
5. How important is it for teachers to use *discipline* in the classroom?
6. Should schools *penalize* students who are caught *wrestling* in the hallway?

# Spanking *on* trial

1 It was his wife's birthday and David Peterson had taken a break from the drive home to celebrate at a restaurant in London, Ontario. With him was his whole family – wife Paula, five-year-old daughter Rachel, and son William, two – fresh from a vacation in Niagara Falls. But Rachel was acting up, refusing to stop wrestling with her brother. When Peterson and his kids went back to the car to fetch a present for their mother, Rachel went over the line. She pushed her brother out of the car to the parking lot asphalt, then slammed the door on his fingers when he tried to get back in. Angered, Peterson did what parents have done with insolent children for centuries: He spanked her. But Marlene Timperio, a mother of a six-year-old boy, saw it all. Noting the Illinois license plate on Peterson's vehicle, Timperio confronted the American, telling him: "This is not what we do in Canada." And then she called the police.

2 So began David Peterson's ordeal, which included a night in a London jail and months of legal headaches, culminating in his trial and acquittal last week on charges of assault. "We were just passing through," the 39-year-old told reporters after the verdict in London, "and we stepped in it, so to speak."

3 Indeed. There are few more contentious issues in parenting – to spank or not to spank? And the Peterson case has only added fuel to the long-standing debate. At the heart of the debate is Section 43 of the Canadian Criminal Code. It allows parents, teachers, and guardians to use "force by way of correction toward a pupil or child . . . if the force does not exceed what is reasonable under the circumstance." During last week's trial, Peterson's lawyer, Michael Menear, argued that the section protected parents who "honestly believe" they are teaching their children proper behavior and do not inflict injury in the process.

4 In his ruling, Mr. Justice John Menzies of the Ontario Court's Provincial Division said he was convinced the Petersons were "responsible, reasonable, and caring parents," and that the spanking of Rachel was not excessive. Menzies added that the testimony of Timperio – who acknowledged that she opposes physical discipline – "brings into sharp focus the different views in society on the subject of child discipline." Still, he added, "this is not a court of social justice, but of the law."

5 But to many child experts and family workers, that law does not go far enough in protecting children. Dr. Elliott Barker, a psychiatrist who treats violent offenders, says that spanking can have "enormous costs" for both individuals and society. "To have the person you are most dependent on turn on you is a psychological blow you don't forget," says Barker. Children, he adds, will come to "believe that spanking is good, and they go on and spank their own kids."

6 After the trial last week, Paula Peterson declined to say whether she and her husband will continue to spank their children. "That's a decision my husband and I will make," she said. Both parents said that they had no hard feelings about Canadians, nor about the debate that has raged around that day in the parking lot.

Adapted from *Maclean's*.

## Before you read

**Check (✔) the information you think you will read about in the text.**

_____ 1. the behavior of the child who was spanked

_____ 2. the name of the person who called the police

_____ 3. the law the parent was accused of breaking

_____ 4. the reasons why parents shouldn't spank

_____ 5. the names of experts who support spanking

## Reading

**Scan the text to check your predictions. Then read the whole text.**

## After you read

**A** **Check (✔) the correct statement.**

_____ 1. The writer supports spanking.

_____ 2. The writer opposes spanking.

_____ 3. The writer doesn't express an opinion.

**B** **Find the words in *italics* in the reading. Then match each word with its meaning.**

_b_ 1. *ordeal* (par. 2)       a. freedom from criminal charges

_____ 2. *culminating* (par. 2)       b. a difficult experience

_____ 3. *acquittal* (par. 2)       c. refused

_____ 4. *contentious* (par. 3)       d. attack suddenly

_____ 5. *turn on* (par. 5)       e. a sudden shock with damaging effects

_____ 6. *blow* (par. 5)       f. ending

_____ 7. *declined* (par. 6)       g. causing disagreement

**C** **Number the information in the order it is mentioned, from 1 (first) to 6 (last).**

_____ a. the judge's decision

_____ b. the problems with laws that protect children

_1_ c. the story that caused the trial

_____ d. the main argument in the Peterson trial

_____ e. the Peterson's feelings about what happened

_____ f. the problems the Petersons had as a result of the spanking

**D** **Answer these questions.**

1. Do you think it is acceptable to spank a child? Why or why not?
2. Do you think Marlene Timperio was right or wrong to call the police? Why?
3. What is the most effective way for parents to punish two-year-olds? Six-year-olds? Nine-year-olds? Thirteen-year-olds? Seventeen-year-olds?

# The Letter

1    Her mother read the letter standing in the middle of the hut with one hand on her forehead. While she read her lips moved rapidly, her eyes blinked severely and often. Finished, she sat down on the edge of a chair, dangled the letter in her hand for a moment, then sighed and took off her glasses. "Surely not," she said in Japanese.

2    She set the glasses in her lap wearily, placed the letter on top of them, and pressed against her eyes with both palms.

3    "The neighborhood boy," she said aloud. "The one who taught her how to swim."

4    Now she stood with this letter in her hand – a letter a boy had sent to her daughter about love. The depth of her deceit became vivid to Fujiko, and she felt in herself a mother's rage at the weight of this betrayal.

5    She reminded herself to behave with dignity no matter what the circumstances, a worthy lesson passed down from her grandmother. *Giri* was her grandmother's word for it – it could not be precisely translated into English – and it meant doing what one had to do quietly and with an entirely stoic demeanor. Fujiko sat back and cultivated in herself the spirit of quiet dignity that would be necessary in confronting Hatsue. She breathed deeply and shut her eyes.

6    Well, she told herself, she would have a talk with Hatsue when the girl came back from wandering aimlessly around the camp. She would put an end to this business.

7    At this moment Hatsue came through the door, her face reddened by the cold outside, and tugged the scarf from her head. When the door had shut Fujiko reached behind her and handed Hatsue the letter. "Here," she spat. "Your mail. I don't know how you could have been so deceitful. I'll never understand it, Hatsue."

8    She had planned to discuss the matter right there and then, but she understood suddenly that the strength of her bitterness might prevent her from saying what she really meant. "You will not write again to this boy or accept his letters," she said sternly from the doorway.

9    The girl sat with the letter in her hand, tears gathering in her eyes. "I'm sorry," Hatsue said. "Forgive me, Mother. I've deceived you and I've always known it."

10    "Deceiving me," said Fujiko in Japanese, "is only half of it, daughter. You have deceived yourself, too."

11    Then Fujiko went out into the wind. She walked to the post office and told the clerk there to hold all mail for the Imada family. From now on, she herself would come for it. It should be handed to her only.

12    That afternoon she sat and wrote her own letter addressed to the boy's parents. She showed it to Hatsue when it was folded and ready to go into its envelope, then took it from her daughter's lap and ripped it neatly down the middle. "Write your own letter," she said in Japanese. "Tell him the truth about things. Put all of this in your history. Tell him the truth so you can move forward. Put this boy away now."

13    In the morning Fujiko took Hatsue's letter to the post office and paid the postage on it. She licked the envelope shut herself and, because the notion took hold of her suddenly – a kind of caprice and nothing more – she pressed the stamp on upside down before putting the letter in the mailbox.

Adapted from *Snow Falling On Cedars.*

> **READING TIP**    Sometimes the meaning of a word precedes the word. For example, in paragraph 13, the meaning of *caprice* is a *notion* [that] *took hold of her suddenly.*

## Before you read

**Look at the picture on the opposite page and these phrases from the text. What do you think happens in the story?**

| | | |
|---|---|---|
| "The neighborhood boy" | behave with dignity | "Forgive me." |
| this betrayal | put an end to this business | "Write your own letter." |
| a mother's rage | "I've deceived you." | letter in the mailbox |

## Reading

**Scan the text to check your prediction. Then read the whole text.**

## After you read

**A** **What is the tone of the text? Check (✔) the correct answer.**

———— 1. humorous     ———— 3. cheerful

———— 2. serious     ———— 4. sarcastic

**B** **Who does "she" refer to in the statements? Write Fujiko (*F*) or Hatsue (*H*).**

_H_ 1. She received a letter from a boy.

———— 2. She read the letter the boy wrote.

———— 3. She was angry.

———— 4. She was apologetic.

———— 5. She wrote a letter to the boy's family.

———— 6. She wrote a letter to the boy.

———— 7. She tore up the letter.

———— 8. She mailed the letter.

**C** **Answer the questions.**

1. How old do you think Hatsue is?
2. What time of year do you think it is?
3. What do you think the boy wrote in his letter?
4. What do you think Fujiko's character is like?
5. What do you think Hatsue's character is like?

**D** **Answer these questions.**

1. Do you think Fujiko was right to forbid her daughter from communicating with the boy? Why or why not?
2. What do you think Hatsue wrote in her letter?
3. Do fathers and mothers differ in the way they punish children? If so, how?

Left margin tabs:
edicting

canning

ecognizing ne

nderstanding ference ords

aking ferences

elating eading to ersonal xperience

# Schools take the fun out of suspension

1   Suspension just isn't what it used to be. Once, frustrated school officials could be sure that if they kicked a misbehaving student out of school, the student's angry and embarrassed parents would do the rest in terms of punishment.

2   But these days, too many parents are working, while others couldn't care less, to be effective jailers. For some students, suspension has become another holiday, all the sweeter because everyone else is in class.

3   Now, several principals in Ventura County are having second thoughts about the whole concept of suspension. They are revamping discipline policies and endorsing a revolutionary approach to punishment – instead of sending students home to the living room couch and daytime TV, they are keeping more troublemakers at school. Students who break school rules are still suspended, but are exiled on campus, where they catch up on homework, write personal goals, or clean up the school.

4   "It's not as fun to be at school as it is to be at home," said Ventura County official Miles Weiss. "And if you are a delinquent or you misbehave at school, you should suffer a consequence, not a reward."

5   Administrators are also concerned about teens falling behind in school. "We want to keep students in school because that's our business," said principal Bob La Belle. "We don't want the students to fall further behind, and penalize them unfairly for what may have happened in one period." He said on-campus suspension prevents the "snowball effect," when a student who gets in trouble in one class is sent home for a few days and ends up behind in all six classes.

6   In several schools, teachers or campus supervisors watch over suspended students. Some schools call their on-campus suspension classes "opportunity rooms." Educators say it's a good name, underscoring the idea that these are places where students have the opportunity to turn their lives around. "Behavior is an outward sign of an inner problem in school," said school superintendent Chuck Weis. "Suspension can give us an opportunity to work on that real underlying problem."

7   Middle school students from Ventura are sent to a special "suspension school" held on Fridays at Ventura College. They spend from 8 A.M. to 2 P.M. there, involved in activities aimed at controlling their anger, boosting their self-esteem, and improving their attitude toward school. In return, the suspension doesn't show up on their school record.

8   At 8:15 A.M. on a recent Friday, teacher Peter Shedlosky asked the students to introduce themselves: their names, grades, schools, and reason for suspension. A few kids' voices cracked as they took their turns reciting their transgressions: "I got kicked out of class. I pushed this guy. I beat up some kid. I got in a fight."

9   Ventura educators say having the suspension school on a college campus also motivates the students to improve their behavior and grades. During the day, they take a tour of the college campus, look through the college catalog, and talk about careers.

10   Westlake High School's on-campus suspension program serves both students and staff. After spending all morning in various study hall classrooms, the students are handed trash bags and ordered to work. As they traverse the hillside and the parking lot picking up coffee cups, soda cans, and fast-food bags, a few classmates pass by, pointing and laughing at the trash collectors.

Adapted from *The Los Angeles Times*.

lating to the
pic

anning

cognizing
rpose

essing
eaning from
ntext

lating
ading to
rsonal
xperience

## Before you read

**Check (✔) the statements you agree with.**

_____ 1. Parents should punish children who get in trouble at school.

_____ 2. Schools should punish students who misbehave.

_____ 3. Students who behave badly should be suspended from school.

_____ 4. Students who behave badly should do extra work at school.

_____ 5. Students who break rules should spend their suspension at home.

## Reading

**Scan the text to find out which statements Ventura educators agree with.
Then read the whole text.**

## After you read

**A** **Check (✔) the writer's main purpose in writing the text.**

_____ 1. to convince parents to support school officials' decisions

_____ 2. to describe the benefits of on-campus suspension programs

_____ 3. to inform educators of some modern punishment techniques

**B** **Find the words in *italics* in the reading. Then match each word with its meaning.**

__c__ 1. *revamping* (par. 3)      a. separated from others

_____ 2. *endorsing* (par. 3)      b. move across

_____ 3. *exiled* (par. 3)      c. changing and improving

_____ 4. *delinquent* (par. 4)      d. emphasizing

_____ 5. *underscoring* (par. 6)      e. a person who behaves badly

_____ 6. *transgressions* (par. 8)      f. supporting

_____ 7. *traverse* (par. 10)      g. actions that break rules

**C** **Answer these questions.**

1. Who should punish a student who gets into trouble at school, the student's
   parents or school officials? Why?
2. What kinds of misbehavior should a student be punished for? What kinds of
   behaviors should teachers ignore?
3. Which on-campus suspension activity do you think is most effective? Why?
   a. cleaning up the school
   b. spending all morning in study
      hall
   c. becoming familiar with a college
      campus
   d. talking about careers
   e. learning to control anger and
      boost self-esteem
   f. writing personal goals

## Vocabulary expansion

**A** Complete the chart with the missing words.

| | Adjective | Noun | Verb |
|---|---|---|---|
| 1. | *confrontational* | confrontation | |
| 2. | | deceit | |
| 3. | | discipline | |
| 4. | effective | | |
| 5. | | | exceed |
| 6. | | | penalize |
| 7. | | punishment | *punish* |
| 8. | | suspension | |

**B** Read the sentences. Write the parts of speech of the missing words. Then complete the sentences with words from the chart in exercise A. (Note: In some cases, more than one word is correct.)

1. Driving without a license is a <u>*punishable*</u> offense.
   <br>                          *adj.*

2. If we _____ you from school, you won't be able to return for one week.

3. Many people think there should be a stronger _____ for cheating on exams.

4. Students who don't go to school will face _____ action.

5. He tried to _____ the police by saying he didn't own the car he was driving.

6. Drivers who _____ the speed limit near a school have to pay a large fine.

7. The criminal was _____ by an angry crowd.

8. We are going to study the _____ of our policy to see how well it works.

## Punishment and you

Work in groups. Number the offenses from 1 (least serious) to 8 (most serious). Then think of a suitable punishment for each one.

| _____ arson[1] | _____ cheating in school | _____ littering[3] | _____ shoplifting[4] |
|---|---|---|---|
| _____ bank robbery | _____ euthanasia[2] | _____ lying | _____ speeding |

[1] setting a fire in order to damage or destroy something, especially a building
[2] killing someone who is very ill to end his or her suffering
[3] throwing out pieces of paper and other small objects in public places
[4] taking things from a store without paying for them

# 7 Loss

UNIT

You are going to read three texts about loss. First, answer the questions in the boxes.

READING 1

## Death & superstition

Read from this website to find out how traditions in one part of the world mark the passing of a loved one.

1. What colors do people in mourning usually wear in your country?
2. What do people in your culture believe happens to the soul after death?
3. What do widows do after their husbands die? What about widowers?

READING 2

## Chapter Two

What do people do to remember someone who dies? This scene from a play shows how one man deals with the loss of his wife.

1. What can a person do to forget the loss of a spouse?
2. Should someone who has lost a spouse move to a new home?
3. Is it appropriate for someone in mourning to laugh and try to forget?

READING 3

## Funeral Blues; The Chariot

Two renowned poets write about the end of life.

1. How do people usually react to the loss of a loved one?
2. In your culture, is death viewed as a beginning or an ending?
3. What are common symbols of death in your culture?

## Vocabulary

**Find out the meanings of the words in *italics*. Then check (✔) the statements that are true about your country.**

_____ 1. People send *condolence* cards or letters.
_____ 2. There are *funeral processions*.
_____ 3. Hearses are used to transport *coffins*.
_____ 4. People honor the memory of their *late* parents.
_____ 5. It is acceptable for people to *grieve* in public.
_____ 6. There are special days when people visit the *graves* of family members.

# Death & superstition

1 A solemn funeral procession slowly winds its way deep into the hills of Kentucky. Six men carry a homemade coffin on their shoulders. Behind is a grieving widow and children, followed by friends and family. There are no sleek, black hearses here, no somber men in dark suits. But this is how folks in Appalachia have buried their dead for hundreds of years. Bearing the coffin to the family cemetery is the last act in a string of traditions.

2 Traditions in Appalachia and the American South are sometimes bound in superstition. The moment that a person dies, a whole series of customs begins to speed the departed's trip to the hereafter, and to insure the well-being of those left behind. A century ago, these rituals were commonplace. Today, however, they are practiced in only some areas.

3 Take, for instance, beliefs about what happens to the soul. Some people believed that the soul remained with the body 24 hours after death. Members of the family, or friends of the deceased, often chose to "sit up" with the body to keep the soul company.

4 While the body was still in the house, certain precautions were taken to insure the welfare of the living. For example, the body was always laid out on the first floor of the house, never on an upper floor. If a step squeaked while the body was still under the roof, there would be a death in the family within a year. Likewise, all clocks were stopped immediately after a death. If a clock stopped on its own, another death would occur shortly.

5 The time of day a person died dictated when the grave was dug. If a person died at night or early in the morning, for example, the grave was dug after noon on the following day. It was bad luck to leave a freshly excavated grave open all night.

6 Digging the grave was a solemn task reserved for family and friends. They dug the grave and filled it up after the funeral. Graves always faced the east toward the rising sun, the symbol of resurrection.

7 After the burial of her husband, the grieving widow was expected to enter a period of mourning. The traditional mourning garb, of course, was black. She gave away all her colored clothing because that was considered good luck.

8 The widow also faced another set of restrictions. She could not court again until a year after the death of her husband, and could not marry for two years after that. The widow was required to visit the grave of her late husband at least four times a week during mourning. She could not speak to another man, unless it was a member of her family or the preacher, until the grave was filled. She could not sing any song, unless it was a hymn, and she could not participate in any kind of recreation. She was forbidden to eat cake, pie, or candy. Nor was she allowed to sip any sweet drink except coffee.

9 If a widow mourned for more than one year, it was bad luck. With restrictions like that hanging over her head, I would dare say that one year of serious lament was more than sufficient.

Adapted from *www.va.essortment.com/deathsuperstiti_rxzf.htm*.

ing previous
owledge

imming

cognizing
nilarity in
eaning

derstanding
tails

lating
ading to
rsonal
perience

## Before you read

Look at the picture on the opposite page. Where do you think it was taken?

## Reading

Skim the text to check your answer. Then read the whole text.

## After you read

**A** Match each word or phrase with a word or phrase that is similar in meaning.

_d_    1. *somber* (par. 1)           a. *carry* (par. 1)

_____ 2. *bearing* (par. 1)          b. *mourning* (pars. 7, 8)

_____ 3. *string* (par. 1)             c. *deceased* (par. 3)

_____ 4. *customs* (par. 2)         d. *solemn* (pars. 1, 6)

_____ 5. *departed* (par. 2)        e. *traditions* (par. 2)

_____ 6. *welfare* (par. 4)          f. *series* (par. 2)

_____ 7. *under the roof* (par. 4)    g. *well-being* (par. 2)

_____ 8. *excavated* (par. 5)       h. *in the house* (par. 4)

_____ 9. *garb* (par. 7)             i. *dug* (par. 5)

_____ 10. *lament* (par. 9)         j. *clothing* (par. 7)

**B** In Appalachia, are these events considered good luck or bad luck?
Check (✔) the correct column.

| | Good luck | Bad Luck |
|---|---|---|
| 1. People leave the body alone during the first 24 hours after death. | | ✓ |
| 2. People go upstairs while the body is still in the house. | | |
| 3. A clock stops working in the house where the body is. | | |
| 4. The grave faces the direction of the rising sun. | | |
| 5. People dig a grave in the afternoon for a funeral the next day. | | |
| 6. A widow gives away all her clothing that is not black. | | |
| 7. A widow mourns for three years. | | |

**C** Answer these questions.

1. What superstitions are associated with death in your country?
2. Do death rituals vary in different parts of your country? If so, what examples can you give?
3. If foreign visitors asked about your country's rituals after someone dies, what would you say?

# Chapter Two

**Marvin Neil Simon** (1927–) *Born in the Bronx, New York, Neil Simon quickly established himself as America's most successful playwright. Following the death of his wife in 1973, Simon went on to write* Chapter Two, *which was considered by many critics to be his finest play to that date.*

1     LEO  . . . What are you reading?

GEORGE  My mail.

LEO  Anything interesting?

GEORGE  Not unless you like letters of condolence. I thought I answered my last one when I left. You want to listen to something, Leo?

LEO  George, you just got home. You're tired. Why don't you defrost the bathroom, take a bath?

GEORGE  Just one letter: "Dear Mr. Schneider, My name is
10         Mary Ann Patterson. We've never met, but I did know your late wife, Barbara, casually. I work at Sabrina's, where she used to come to have her hair cut. She was so beautiful and one of the warmest people I've ever met. It seems I always used to tell her my troubles, and she always found some terrific thing to say to cheer me up. I will miss her smiling face and the way she used to come bouncing into the shop like a little girl. I feel lucky to have known her. I just wanted to return a little of her good cheer. God bless you and keep you. Mary Ann Patterson." (*He puts down the letter.* LEO *looks at him, knowing not to intrude on this moment.*) What the hell did I read *that* for?

20    LEO  It's very nice. It's a sweet letter, George.

GEORGE  Barbara knew a whole world of people I never knew . . . She knew that Ricco, the mailman, was a birdwatcher in Central Park, and that Vince, the butcher in Gristede's, painted miniature portraits of cats every weekend in his basement on Staten Island . . . She talked to people all year long that I said hello to on Christmas.

LEO  I think you could have used another month in Europe.

GEORGE  You mean, I was supposed to come home and forget I had a wife for twelve years? It doesn't work that way, Leo. It was, perhaps, the dumbest trip I ever took in my whole life. London was bankrupt, Italy was on strike, France hated me . . . Why do Americans go to grief-stricken Europe when they're trying to get over being stricken with grief?

30    LEO  Beats me. I always thought you could have just as rotten a time here in America.

GEORGE  What am I going to do about this apartment, Leo?

LEO  My advice? Move. Find a new place for yourself.

GEORGE  It was very spooky in London . . . I kept walking around the streets looking for Barbara – Harrod's King's Road, Portobello . . . Sales clerks would say, "See what you want, sir?" and I'd say, "No, she's not here." I know it's crazy, Leo, but I really thought to myself, It's a joke. She's not dead. She's in London waiting for me. She's just playing out this romantic fantasy: The whole world thinks she's gone, but we meet clandestinely in London, move into a flat, disappear from everyone and live out our lives in secret! . . . She would have thought of something like that, you know.

40    LEO  But she didn't. *You* did.

GEORGE  In Rome I got sore at her – I mean really mad. How dare she do a thing like this to me? I would *never* do a thing like that to her. Never! Like a nut, walking up the Via Veneto one night, cursing my dead wife.

LEO  In Italy, they probably didn't pay attention.

GEORGE  In Italy, they agree with you. (*He shrugs*) Okay, Leo, my sweet baby brother, I'm back . . . Chapter Two in the life of George Schneider. Where the hell do I begin?

From *Chapter Two.*

dicting

anning

essing
aning from
ntext

aking
erences

elating
ading to
rsonal
perience

## Before you read

**Read the backround information about this scene. Then answer the questions below.**

*After the death of his wife, George Schneider, 42, spent a month in Europe. He has just returned home. His brother, Leo, has picked him up at the airport, and they have just entered the apartment George shared with his late wife. The first thing George does is look through the mail.*

1. What do you think George did on his trip to Europe?
2. What do you think he finds in the mail?

## Reading

**Scan the text to check your predictions. Then read the whole text.**

## After you read

**A** **Find the words in *italics* in the reading. Circle the meaning of each word.**

1. *stricken* (line 26)
   a. (suffering greatly)
   b. knowing about
   c. refusing to work
2. *rotten* (line 27)
   a. enjoyable
   b. interesting
   c. terrible
3. *spooky* (line 31)
   a. expensive
   b. frightening
   c. boring
4. *clandestinely* (line 35)
   a. slowly
   b. patiently
   c. secretly
5. *nut* (line 40)
   a. a kind person
   b. a strange person
   c. a ghost
6. *cursing* (line 41)
   a. wishing things were different
   b. saying bad words at
   c. talking to oneself

**B** **Check (✔) the statements that are true.**

  ✓   1. George got letters of condolence before he went on his trip.
_____ 2. Leo thinks George should do things to forget his wife's death.
_____ 3. Leo didn't like George's wife.
_____ 4. Barbara was friendlier than George.
_____ 5. George loved his wife very much.
_____ 6. George didn't miss his wife until he returned home.
_____ 7. George is excited about the changes in his life.

**C** **Answer these questions.**

1. Why do you think the play is called *Chapter Two*?
2. What do you think George does next?
3. What advice would you give George?

# Funeral Blues

**Wystan Hugh Auden** (1907–1973) *Generally considered one of the most important poets of the twentieth century, the English-born writer has had a major literary influence on both sides of the Atlantic. The 1930 publication of his collection* Poems *established him as the leading voice of a new generation.*

1    Stop all the clocks, cut off the telephones,
Prevent the dog from barking with a juicy bone,
Silence the pianos and with muffled drum
Bring out the coffin, let the mourners come.

2    Let aeroplanes circle moaning overhead
Scribbling on the sky the message He Is Dead,
Put crepe bows round the white necks of the public doves,
Let the traffic policemen wear black cotton gloves.

3    He was my North, my South, my East and West,
My working week and my Sunday rest,
My moon, my midnight, my talk, my song;
I thought that love would last for ever: I was wrong.

4    The stars are not wanted now: put out every one;
Pack up the moon and dismantle the sun;
Pour away the ocean and sweep up the wood;
For nothing now can ever come to any good.

# The Chariot

**Emily Dickinson** (1830–1886) *America's best-known female poet, Emily Dickinson is one of the most innovative writers in nineteenth-century American literature. Her use of metaphors to deal with issues of death, faith, immortality, and nature significantly influenced modern poetry.*

1    Because I could not stop for Death,
He kindly stopped for me;
The carriage held but just ourselves
And Immortality.

2    We slowly drove, he knew no haste,
And I had put away
My labor, and my leisure too,
For his civility.

3    We passed the school where children played,
Their lessons scarcely done;
We passed the fields of gazing grain,
We passed the setting sun.

4    We paused before a house that seemed
A swelling of the ground;
The roof was scarcely visible,
The cornice but a mound.

5    Since then 'tis centuries; but each
Feels shorter than the day
I first surmised the horses' heads
Were toward eternity.

> **READING TIP**    Each line of English poetry usually begins with a capital letter. For example, in verse 2, line 8 of "The Chariot," *For* is capitalized because it is at the beginning of the line, not because it begins a new sentence.

## Before you read

edicting

Look at the titles of the poems and the pictures on the opposite page. Predict what each poem is about. (Note: Blues is a slow, sad type of music or a mood of sadness. A chariot is a two-wheeled vehicle pulled by a horse.)

## Reading

kimming

Skim the text to check your predictions. Then read the whole text.

## After you read

uessing eaning from ontext

**A** Find the words in the reading that match each definition.

1. ___muffled___ : made quieter and less clear ("Funeral Blues," verse 1)
2. _____ : making a long low sound of pain ("Funeral Blues," verse 2)
3. _____ : birds ("Funeral Blues," verse 2)
4. _____ : the state of living forever ("The Chariot," verse 1)
5. _____ : great speed ("The Chariot," verse 2)
6. _____ : polite behavior ("The Chariot," verse 2)
7. _____ : decoration at the top of a building ("The Chariot," verse 4)
8. _____ : guessed ("The Chariot," verse 5)

nderstanding ain ideas

**B** Circle the correct answers.

1. Who died in "Funeral Blues"?
   a. someone famous
   b. someone the poet loved
2. What is the poet's reaction to the death?
   a. Life isn't worth living.
   b. Life will go on.
3. What is "The Chariot" about?
   a. the fear of death
   b. the peacefulness of death

4. What does the chariot represent?
   a. Death taking the narrator into eternity
   b. the narrator's memories of life
5. What is the main idea of "The Chariot"?
   a. Death is nothing to be afraid of.
   b. We must remember those who leave.

hyming

**C** Fill in the blanks with rhyming words from the poems.

| Funeral Blues | | | |
|---|---|---|---|
| 1. telephone | _bone_ | 5. West | _____ |
| 2. drum | _____ | 6. song | _____ |
| 3. overhead | _____ | 7. one | _____ |
| 4. doves | _____ | 8. wood | _____ |

| The Chariot | |
|---|---|
| 9. me | _____ |
| 10. done | _____ |
| 11. ground | _____ |
| 12. day | _____ |

elating ading to ersonal perience

**D** Answer these questions.

1. Which poem do you prefer? Why?
2. How long do you think the first poet grieved? Why?
3. Do you agree with the second poet that death should not be feared? Why or why not?

## Vocabulary expansion

**A** *Homographs* are words that have the same spelling but different meanings. They also may have different pronunciations. Circle the homographs in the pairs of sentences below. Then choose the correct meaning of each circled word from below.

| | | |
|---|---|---|
| _l_ | 1. The (winds) are strong today. | a. pulls into pieces |
| ___ | 2. The road winds through the valley. | b. jumped headfirst into water |
| ___ | 3. The dove is a symbol of peace. | c. a black material used for writing |
| ___ | 4. The swimmer dove into the water. | d. moves in a curving manner |
| ___ | 5. They say that cats have nine lives. | e. decorative knots |
| ___ | 6. Kate lives in London. | f. periods between birth and death |
| ___ | 7. The gifts have large bows on them. | g. walk in front, with others following |
| ___ | 8. Taro bows when he greets people. | h. bends forward to show respect |
| ___ | 9. The sad child wept tears. | i. makes one's home somewhere |
| ___ | 10. This material tears easily. | j. drops of liquid that flow from the eye |
| ___ | 11. Men will lead the funeral possession. | k. a type of white bird |
| ___ | 12. Pencils contain lead. | l. movements of the air outside |

**B** Circle the correct answers about the homographs from exercise A.

1. In 1, *winds* rhymes with **minds** / **(twins.)**
2. In 2, *winds* rhymes with **minds** / **twins**.

3. In 3, *dove* rhymes with **love** / **stove**.
4. In 4, *dove* rhymes with **love** / **stove**.

5. In 5, *lives* rhymes with **fives** / **gives**.
6. In 6, *lives* rhymes with **fives** / **gives**.

7. In 7, *bows* rhymes with **knows** / **cows**.
8. In 8, *bows* rhymes with **knows** / **cows**.

9. In 9, *tears* rhymes with **fears** / **wears**.
10. In 10, *tears* rhymes with **fears** / **wears**.

11. In 11, *lead* rhymes with **need** / **red**.
12. In 12, *lead* rhymes with **need** / **red**.

## Loss and you

Look at Reading 2 on page 52 again. Imagine you went to high school or college with George's late wife. Write George a letter of condolence. Include memories about her in your letter.

**U N I T**

# 8 Memory

You are going to read three texts about memory. First, answer the questions in the boxes.

## Can you believe what you see?

Read this newspaper article to discover whether your memory is as accurate as you think it is.

1. Can police trust eyewitness's reports?
2. Have you ever witnessed an accident? Do you remember the details?
3. Do you know anyone who can remember everything?

## Man weds the wife he forgot

This newspaper article describes how complete memory loss affected one man and those around him.

1. What causes memory loss?
2. What do you think a woman would do if her husband didn't remember her?
3. How would you feel if you suddenly couldn't remember anything?

## Repeat after me: Memory takes practice

What can you do to improve your memory? Read this newspaper article for some answers.

1. What do you do to help you remember things?
2. What is easy for you to remember? What is difficult?
3. Do you think students who have a good memory do better in school?

### Vocabulary

**Find out the meanings of the words in *italics*. Then check (✔) the statements that are true about you.**

_____ 1. I know someone whose memory has *diminished* with age.

_____ 2. I occasionally have a memory *lapse*.

_____ 3. It's hard to remember things when I have a lot *on my mind*.

_____ 4. I can *recall* some things better than others.

_____ 5. I *retain* information better if I learn it earlier in the day.

_____ 6. I can *retrieve* memories from certain periods of my life better than others.

# Can you believe what you see?

1 A crime's been committed. The police are sure they have the right guy in custody. After all, they have an eyewitness. But should they be so sure? "No," claim psychologists who have studied eyewitness testimony.

2 Daniel Wright, a psychologist at Sussex University, has found that when witnesses are given misleading information after an incident, some will adapt their memories to accommodate this new information. In one experiment, 40 students looked at a picture book showing the story of two men meeting at a pool hall and of a woman later stealing one man's wallet. Each student studied the book on his or her own.

3 Without any of the volunteers knowing, half of the group had slightly different information from the other half. Twenty students saw a picture book showing the woman loitering outside the pool hall on her own before the crime. The other half saw a picture of her loitering with an accomplice.

4 When questioned afterwards, on their own, about whether the woman had an accomplice, 39 of the 40 students got it right. Then the students were paired off so that, in each pair, only one had seen the picture book featuring the accomplice and one had viewed the picture book without the accomplice.

5 Each pair was asked to discuss what they knew, and to answer the question jointly: Did the woman have an accomplice?

6 Since the members of each pair had seen different scenarios, none of them should have reached agreement. In fact, fifteen pairs reached a compromise. In other words, 15 witnesses were swayed by what their partner had told them. (Eight pairs reported no accomplice, while seven reported the opposite).

7 One reason why our memories change is that, when given information, we use it to fill visual gaps. Wright explains: "Imagine a police officer saying, 'I want to ask you about the collision between the red car and green car. Was there a Yield sign at the junction?' If you can't remember the colors, you may use this information to fill the gaps and you may later remember the cars being red and green."

8 False memories can even be planted from scratch. Give people a selection of childhood memories, three of which are true and one is false (the experimenters collaborate with parents), and many subjects will come to believe, quite strongly, that all were genuine experiences. "You can convince adult volunteers that they were lost in a shopping mall as a child even though parents confirm that such an event never took place," he says.

9 So how can the police get the best out of eyewitnesses? Wright says that the best cases are where observers have been able to watch a culprit for a while rather than seeing them for a fleeting moment. All interviews should be conducted as soon as possible, with witnesses freely recalling what happened and not subjected to leading questions.

10 "If you give memory too much of a helping hand, memories will appear, whether they are true or not," Wright says.

Adapted from *The Times (London)*.

## Before you read

Check (✔) the statements you think are true.

_____ 1. Witnesses sometimes change their stories when they hear new information.

_____ 2. Adults can be convinced that invented events happened to them as children.

_____ 3. Witnesses' memories are affected by how long they observe something.

_____ 4. It doesn't matter how long after a crime an eyewitness is interviewed.

## Reading

Scan the text to check your answers. Then read the whole text.

## After you read

**A** Identify which sentence in each pair is the main idea and which is the supporting idea. Write main idea (*M*) or supporting idea (*S*).

1. _*M*_ a. Witnesses adapt their memories to include new information.

   _*S*_ b. Psychologists have studied eyewitness testimony.

2. _____ a. If a police officer mentions red and green cars, you may remember them.

   _____ b. We use new information to fill visual gaps.

3. _____ a. You can convince adults of childhood events that never occurred.

   _____ b. False memories can be created from scratch.

**B** Complete the chart with information about the experiment.

| | |
|---|---|
| 1. Number of people in the experiment: | 40 |
| 2. Number correct in part one of the experiment: | |
| 3. Task of pairs in part two of the experiment: | |
| 4. Reason pairs should not reach an agreement: | |
| 5. Number of pairs reporting an accomplice: | |
| 6. Number of pairs reporting no accomplice: | |
| 7. Findings of the experiment: | |

**C** Answer these questions.

1. What should the police do when the only proof is eyewitness testimony? Why?
2. Do you remember things that happened to you as a child? Would other family members agree with your memory of the event?
3. What happened the first time this class met? Do your classmates agree?

# Man weds the wife he forgot

1 To Ken Howell, the last four decades are a closed book.

2 A brain tumor caused such a catastrophic memory loss that he was left believing he was still a teenager in the 1950s. He thought modern cars looked like space ships, had never heard of the Kennedy assassination or the Beatles, and was shocked to learn that Elvis Presley was dead.

3 Worst of all, he did not even know that he was married or that he was the father of three grown children. With infinite care and patience, however, his wife Christine introduced 56-year-old Mr. Howell to life in the twenty-first century, and he fell in love with her all over again.

4 Mrs. Howell said, "We have both had good careers, we have worked hard, had three beautiful children and a lovely home," she said. "The children had all left home and we were looking forward to a wonderful future together when Ken suddenly fell ill.

5 "He had a heavy cold for a while and severe headaches. Eventually things got so bad that he was sent to hospital, and in June of 1997 he slipped into a coma and was diagnosed as having cancer of the brain."

6 Mrs. Howell stayed at his bedside for three months and, miraculously, he recovered. "But when he came out of the coma he did not know who I was," she said. "It was the same with the children; they were strangers to him. When I took him home he was reluctant to come with me but he did. When I told him I was his wife and he said, 'You can't be, you're too old.'"

7 "Worst of all was not remembering me and the children because we had been so close. At first he thought I was nursing him and he had no idea who the children were. He would just send them away when they came to visit."

8 "But softly, softly through videos and photographs, he has clawed back some of his past although he does find it all very upsetting, as you can imagine. One day I managed to get him to watch the video of Karen's wedding. He gave her away and made speeches at all of his children's weddings. Tears came running down his face. He said, 'I want to get married again.' He said he had to do it so he could have a memory of his marriage. It was so romantic."

9 Mr. Howell said, "It has been a very hard three years, especially for Christine and the children. I have found it very hard not remembering things. I cannot remember meeting Christine or getting married or having children – all those wonderful moments in a man's life."

10 "I had to watch a video of man walking on the moon because I just refused to believe Christine when she told me it had happened. The cars people drive these days, the cost of everything, the way houses are, the way people dress and speak, music, color TV, video players and CDs – it's all a bit strange to a man stuck in the late fifties."

11 "I got to thinking that everything I was being told must be true, and I have fallen in love with Christine all over again. I cried with joy when she said she would marry me again."

Adapted from *The Sunday Telegraph.*

## Before you read

edicting

Look at the title on the opposite page. Then check (✔) the information you think you will read about in the text.

_____ 1. After his first wife's death, a man married his childhood sweetheart.

_____ 2. A man married a woman twice because he couldn't remember the first wedding.

_____ 3. A man married a second woman because he didn't remember that he was married.

_____ 4. A man missed his wedding because he forgot he was getting married.

_____ 5. A man had difficulty remembering things all of his life.

_____ 6. A man lost his memory in a car accident.

## Reading

canning

Scan the text to check your predictions. Then read the whole text.

## After you read

uessing eaning from ntext

**A** Find the words in *italics* in the reading. Circle the meaning of each word.

1. *a closed book* (par. 1)
   a. something you can't read
   b. something you know nothing about
   c. something very interesting
   d. someone's life story
2. *slipped into a coma* (par. 5)
   a. fell down
   b. spent time in the hospital
   c. had an operation
   d. became unconscious

3. *reluctant* (par. 6)
   a. not wanting
   b. not able
   c. excited
   d. worried
4. *give her away* (par. 8)
   a. tell her secret
   b. give her a gift
   c. reveal her feelings
   d. present the bride

nderstanding etails

**B** Answer these questions on a separate piece of paper.

1. What was the progression of Ken's illness?

   *He had a heavy cold and severe headaches, went to the hospital, slipped into a coma, and was diagnosed with brain cancer. He came out of the coma with memory loss.*

2. What things surprised him about modern life?
3. What famous people and well-known events could he not remember?
4. What important people in his life could he not remember?
5. What important events in his life could he not remember?

elating eading to ersonal xperience

**C** Answer these questions.

1. Do you know anyone who has lost his or her memory? If so, what happened?
2. What would you do if a spouse or family member lost his or her memory?
3. What would you do if you lost your memory?

# Repeat after me: Memory takes practice

1　Meghan Pierce is a 16-year-old senior whose excellent memory has helped her achieve top grades in high school. But asked which of last year's lessons she is forgetting this summer, she joked, "Everything."

2　It's not the summer sun causing the lapses. Pierce says she's having the most trouble remembering Spanish and history facts, and brain experts say the problem is infrequency of use. Memory lapses, once chiefly the worry of the elderly, have emerged as a source of anxiety among folks of all ages in this era of information overload.

3　"My mom will tell me to do a chore, and I'll walk upstairs to get the vacuum cleaner, and I'll have to walk back downstairs to ask her what I was supposed to do," said Pierce. "There are just so many things on our minds."

4　Researchers say memory can indeed be improved, but the keys to achieving it are simpler than you might think – lots of practice and better organization. Not to mention focus, something that was reinforced to renowned cellist Yo-Yo Ma after he left his $2.5 million, 266-year-old cello in a New York taxi in 1999. (It was recovered.)

5　Misplace keys? Keep them in the same place every day. Forget names? Use word associations. Knowing that someone's name is "Baker" means less than remembering that someone is a baker. Fearful of forgetting an important date? Tell your brain it is relevant and mentally repeat it, again and again.

6　That doesn't mean that it is easy to improve memory – studies by manufacturers of herbs that claim to do so have been challenged by

many leading scientists – or that learning how to better retain certain information makes someone inherently smarter.

7　New research is showing that memories can be diminished by stress and even by physical trauma. Young soccer players who take a lot of headshots report some mild memory problems.

8　Besides, experts say, forgetting some things is normal. "We function so well as human beings because in fact we forget things at a very efficient rate," said neuroscientist James L. Olds. "If we flawlessly remember everything about every aspect of every day, we would have tremendous difficulty given the fact that our brains are limited . . . Forgetting is as important biologically as memory."

9　And forgetting long division over the summer doesn't count because the information isn't really "lost." The foundation has probably been retained in the brain, and it can be easily retrieved with review in the fall, experts said.

10　What students generally lose over the summer are isolated facts not associated with images and not embedded in a larger framework, said Ira B. Black, at the Robert Wood Johnson Medical School in New Jersey. "In a sense, then, you have to care to remember," he said.

11　It is also easier to forget information that is new and different, said psychology professor Alan S. Brown. "If you have been studying English grammar all year, it is less likely to be forgotten than the Spanish which you first started taking in the spring semester."

12　Fifteen-year-old Lyndsey Wilson agreed. "All the stuff they teach in one day I forget. We learned World War II over three weeks, and I remember that."

Adapted from *The Washington Post*.

> **READING TIP**　It is important to identify main ideas and the examples used to support them. For example, *studies by manufacturers of herbs that claim to do so have been challenged by many leading scientists* (par. 6) is evidence that it is not easy to improve memory.

## Before you read

**Mark each statement true (*T*) or false (*F*).**

_____ 1. Only the elderly worry about memory loss.

_____ 2. Even good students forget things.

_____ 3. Students normally forget things over long school vacations.

_____ 4. The amount of time students study doesn't affect their memory of a subject.

_____ 5. Learning to remember information better will make you smarter.

## Reading

**Scan the text to check your answers. Then read the whole text.**

## After you read

**A** | **What do these words refer to?**

1. *her* (par. 1, line 1)  _Meghan Pierce_       4. *it* (par. 5, line 8) _____
2. *it* (par. 4, line 3) _____        5. *it* (par. 9, line 6) _____
3. *It* (par. 4, line 10) _____       6. *that* (par. 12, line 5) _____

**B** | **Find the words in the reading that match each definition.**

1. _____*overload*_____ : too much of something (par. 2)

2. _____ : ways; methods (par. 4)

3. _____ : famous (par. 4)

4. _____ : found (par. 4)

5. _____ : without mistakes (par. 8)

**C** | **Identify which phrases are main ideas and which are supporting ideas. Write main idea (*M*) or supporting idea (*S*). Then write details from the text to support the idea.**

_M_ 1. Reasons for memory lapses *infrequency of use, new and different information, isolated facts*

_____ 2. Comments from students _____

_____ 3. Reasons for memory loss _____

_____ 4. Results of a lack of focus _____

_____ 5. Tips for improving memory in general _____

_____ 6. Tips for remembering specific things _____

**D** | **Answer these questions.**

1. What are (or were) the easiest subjects for you to remember at school?
2. What techniques do you use to help you remember things more effectively?
3. Have you studied something recently that you have already forgotten?
   If so, how long did you study it?

## Vocabulary expansion

**A** **Read the sentences. Then write the phrase in *italics* under the correct heading below.**

1. I *remember* the day I got married *as if it were yesterday*.
2. Jesse's always *been absent-minded*. When he was a child, he couldn't find his shoes; now he never knows where his glasses or his keys are.
3. If I look at my notes right before an exam, it helps *refresh my memory*.
4. I can never remember anybody's birthday; I *have a memory like a sieve*.
5. Ann has forgotten her umbrella again. She *is* really *scatter-brained*.
6. Give me a second. The answer *is on the tip of my tongue*.
7. No matter how much I *rack my brain*, I can't remember where I bought the CD.
8. Look at this picture; maybe it will *jog your memory*.
9. The name *rings a bell*, but I don't really remember him.
10. I can tell the police exactly what happened. The accident is *fresh in my mind*.

| Remember something well | Make someone remember something | Try hard to remember something | Remember something vaguely | Have a bad memory |
|---|---|---|---|---|
| remember . . . as if it were yesterday | | | | |

**B** **Answer the questions.**

1. Do you know anyone who has a memory like a sieve?
2. Are any of your friends scatter-brained?
3. Have you ever had an absent-minded teacher?
4. Can you remember any event from your past as if it were yesterday?
5. What do you do before an exam to refresh your memory?
6. Look at the pictures on page 1 of Unit 1. Do they jog your memory of the unit?

## Memory and you

How good is your memory? Look at the phrases in part A for 30 seconds. Try to remember as many as you can about the picture. Then close your book and write down as many phrases as you can remember. Compare answers with your classmates. Who has the best memory?

UNIT

# 9 Personality

**You are going to read three texts about personality. First, answer the questions in the boxes.**

## READING 1

## What do our possessions say about us?

This newspaper article describes the results of a study linking possessions to personality.

1. What do a person's possessions reveal about his or her personality?
2. Have you ever looked through someone's CD or book collection?
3. What personality traits do you like? What traits do you dislike?

## READING 2

## The role of temperament in shaping individuality

Read this book excerpt to learn how people's temperament and personality affect their behavior.

1. Do you have a predisposition to be happy or sad?
2. Do you think people change as they get older?
3. Why do you think people react differently to the same situation?

## READING 3

## Mind your P's and Q's

How much can you tell about people from their handwriting? Read this magazine article and find out.

1. What does your handwriting look like?
2. Do you know anyone who has very unusual handwriting?
3. Does your handwriting change when you write in a different language? If so, how?

## Vocabulary

**Find out the meanings of the words in the box. Then circle the words that describe you.**

| | | | | |
|---|---|---|---|---|
| aggressive | extroverted | optimistic | self-assured | unconventional |
| boisterous | inhibited | outgoing | self-centered | undependable |
| conscientious | intellectual | restless | sullen | withdrawn |

# What do our possessions say about us?

1 On top of my computer sits a desiccated piranha with a mouthful of razor-sharp teeth. Why is that fish there? To remind me of that wonderful trip to Venezuela? To signal I'm not to be messed with? Maybe it's there because I'm a creative, unconventional individual who refuses to be stifled by the corporate office culture. Or maybe it's because that's what I want people to think.

2 If one little dried-out fish can potentially carry that much information, just think how much could be gleaned from a roomful of possessions. And we are constantly trying to glean. Who hasn't nosed furtively through a CD collection or bookshelf at someone's home to get some measure of our host's personality? "It's a basic human need to want to know what people are like, for all kinds of reasons: Can we trust them? Are they a potential mate?" says Samuel Gosling, assistant professor of psychology. "So, when we're in places where information is rich, we make use of it."

3 Not everything we deduce will be accurate, of course. People may display misleading messages. Someone who's ruthlessly ambitious might adorn his or her office with inspirational posters applauding teamwork. A conservative college kid may flaunt CDs of hip rock stars to appear cool.

4 What's more, observers may guess erroneously from what they see. The fact that I have a two-foot-high in-tray doesn't mean I'm scatterbrained and undependable. And who knows what my co-worker with the welcoming basket of candy and smiley-face pencil is thinking?

5 To find out what people deduce from someone's "social environment" – and whether those deductions are accurate – Gosling enrolled 83 students and 94 office workers in a study. All agreed to have their bedrooms (in the students' case) or offices assessed by observers.

6 Participants were told not to alter anything. And even if they did rush around picking up sweaty socks, "there's a big difference between a tidied room and one that's deeply tidy," Gosling says. "There's only so much you can do in a short time to alphabetize the books and CDs, color-code the stationery, sharpen all your pencils and line them up – things that deeply tidy people do."

7 Each assessor then scored the occupant on a scale of one to seven for five broad personality traits:

· openness to new experiences
· agreeableness
· extroversion
· emotional stability (how calm, relaxed, and self-assured someone is)
· conscientiousness or dependability (whether someone shows up for meetings and pays parking tickets on time)

8 To test the results, Gosling and colleagues compared raters' assessments to ones done by occupants and friends. Raters gleaned a lot in just a few minutes, Gosling says. They weren't great at assessing agreeableness and extroversion, but they were surprisingly adept at scoring someone's dependability and openness to new experiences.

9 Gosling notes that some employers prohibit the personalization of office spaces. Might this damage morale? "The fact that wherever I go I see these expressions of individuality leaking out makes me think it probably isn't a good thing to do." He plans to explore this by having pairs of students decorate each other's living quarters.

10 "What, for instance, would happen if I made you trade your piranha for an angel?" he says. "You'd probably find it very distressing." As, very likely, would anyone who befriended me based on that angel.

Adapted from *The Los Angeles Times*.

**READING TIP** Words in parentheses sometimes define a word in the text. For example, the writer explains *dependability* (par. 7) as *whether someone shows up for meetings and pays parking tickets on time.*

## Before you read

What personality traits can you assess by looking at people's possessions?
Check (✔) your answers.

_____ 1. openness to new experiences

_____ 2. agreeableness

_____ 3. extroversion

_____ 4. dependability

## Reading

Scan the text to check your prediction. Then read the whole text.

**A** ## After you read

Match each word or phrase with a word or phrase that is similar in meaning.

_b_ 1. *desiccated* (par. 1)          a. *display* (par. 3)

_____ 2. *glean* (par. 2, 4)          b. *dried-out* (par. 2)

_____ 3. *adorn* (par. 3)             c. *home* (par. 2)

_____ 4. *flaunt* (par. 3)            d. *find out* (par. 5)

_____ 5. *assess* (par. 5, 8)         e. *score* (par. 7, 8)

_____ 6. *living quarters* (par. 9)   f. *decorate* (par. 9)

**B** Mark each sentence inference (*I*), restatement (*R*), or not in the text (*?*).

_I_ 1. The writer of the text once took a trip to Venezuela.

_____ 2. Ambitious people are not usually interested in teamwork.

_____ 3. In Gosling's study, students assessed the personality traits of office workers.

_____ 4. Participants were not supposed to change the appearance of their rooms.

_____ 5. The assessors were better at scoring some personality traits than others.

_____ 6. The assessors quickly made decisions about personality traits.

_____ 7. People should be allowed to display personal possessions at work.

_____ 8. If people see an angel in somebody's office, they might think the person is nice.

**C** Answer these questions.

1. What kind of possessions do you have? What do you think they say about you?
2. How do you decorate your room or office? What do you think this conveys to others?
3. Do you judge people based on their possessions? Why or why not?

# The role of temperament in shaping individuality

1    Why do I need everything to be completely shipshape? Why am I always getting into battles with my boss and my children? Why is my sister so restless while I'm quite happy to sit home and read? What's wrong with me, or is there something wrong with her? Why am I always so happy while my wife is often sad, even when we're both on vacation? My brother is a much harder worker than I am; how can I match him? Most of us ask ourselves these questions at least occasionally; others concentrate on them almost constantly and spend lots of time and money to come up with answers.

2    Parents know better, and know that their children are born with very definite dispositions. "He was always a quiet little boy," they'll say, or "She was always climbing trees and looking for excitement." Our singularity isn't completely fixed on day one of birth, but we all have an inherent temperament – to be sociable and outgoing or shy and withdrawn.

3    Modern psychologists use the word *temperament* to refer to a person's predisposition to respond to specific events in a specific way. Temperament refers to the style rather than to the content of behavior. We might say that it is the "how" of behavior, not the "what."

4    *Personality,* on the other hand, is the full-blown complex set of reactions that distinguish an individual. We would need to list hundreds of particulars in order to describe a person we know well: slow to anger; tough when provoked; generally calm; reads the sports pages; generous; athletic.

5    Temperament is more general, more basic than the whole complex personality. It concerns whether one does everything slowly or quickly, whether one seeks excitement or sits alone, whether one is highly expressive or inhibited, joyous or sullen. One can be a musician who plays slowly or quickly, with small hand movements or sweeping ones; one can be aggressive in the stock market with a quiet temperament or a boisterous one; one can be a dutiful mother whether one is excitable or calm.

6    Each of us has implicit theories of individuality. We use them not only to type other people ("Joe is an honest person.") but to predict ("Morgan is generous, so I'll ask her if I can borrow a ten."). Belief in the importance of traits and types rests on the assumption that knowing a person's characteristics will tell us something about how that person will behave. Trying to predict how anyone will act, however, is a bit like trying to predict the weather in some random month from now in a random place at a random time.

7    We tend to see how a person behaves and then attribute that behavior to a basic personality trait. Most of us assume that these traits consistently influence others' behavior. We think that someone who is honest never lies to friends, does not cheat, and doesn't steal. But we are so often wrong. Some psychologists question whether people really are consistent enough across situations to make knowledge of traits useful in predicting behavior. This very complexity, however, is probably what keeps most of us interested in each other, as we puzzle over how to piece together an accurate picture of another person.

Adapted from *Roots of the Self*.

dicting

anning

cognizing
rces

essing
aning from
ntext

derstanding
in ideas

lating
ading to
rsonal
perience

## Before you read

**Read the first paragraph on the opposite page. Then check (✔) what you think the text will be about.**

_____ 1. ways the writer can improve himself

_____ 2. personality problems that some people have

_____ 3. effects of personality on behavior

## Reading

**Scan the text to check your predictions. Then read the whole text.**

## After you read

**A** **Where does the text probably come from? Check (✔) the correct answer.**

_____ 1. a book about the science of human behavior

_____ 2. a book about people with personality disorders

_____ 3. a parent's guide to improving family relationships

**B** **Find the words in _italics_ in the reading. Then match each word with its meaning.**

_d_ 1. _shipshape_ (par. 1)      a. details

_____ 2. _inherent_ (par. 2)      b. chance

_____ 3. _particulars_ (par. 4)      c. present at birth

_____ 4. _implicit_ (par. 6)      d. organized

_____ 5. _random_ (par. 6)      e. view as the result

_____ 6. _attribute to_ (par. 7)      f. not expressed

**C** **Write the number of each paragraph next to its main idea.**

_5_ a. This paragraph compares temperament with personality.

_____ b. This paragraph suggests why people are interested in personality traits.

_____ c. This paragraph shows how parents describe their children.

_____ d. This paragraph discusses how people try to predict behavior.

_____ e. This paragraph illustrates differences between people.

_____ f. This paragraph defines personality.

_____ g. This paragraph defines temperament.

**D** **Answer these questions.**

1. How is your temperament similar to that of your family members? How is it different?
2. How is your temperament different from your personality?
3. How would you describe your teacher's personality?

# MIND YOUR P'S AND Q'S

1 As you're gathering love letters from your admirers this Valentine's Day, wouldn't it be nice to know if that special sweetie is Mr. or Ms. Right? While it's not scientific, Graphology – also called handwriting analysis – can provide useful clues about your amour's personality. "In this country, handwriting analysis is considered akin to astrology – something not taken very seriously – but it probably tells us more about a human being than any psychological test," says Ted Widmer, director of the International School of Handwriting Sciences. He provides basic hints for deciphering that love note.

2 Ideally, handwriting analysis should be performed on an unlined page of original writing, not a photocopy or fax. When studying a sample, the first characteristic a graphologist considers is the writer's use of space: "There are universal concepts people in all societies and cultures have regarding the use of space," notes Widmer.

3 **Left and right margins**
The right symbolizes the future and the left represents the past – even in cultures that use the Arabic or Hebrew alphabets and whose writing moves from right to left. In graphology, leaving a narrow right margin suggests a risk-taking person who is unafraid of the future, whereas leaving a narrow left margin implies someone very tied to the past, even fearful of moving on.

4 **Writing that moves uphill or downhill**
"The symbolism of this is revealed in everyday language," says Widmer. "If you're feeling good, you're 'up,' and if you're feeling bad, you're 'down.' Handwriting reflects this." Thus, writing that tends to slope upward from left to right indicates an optimistic attitude, whereas handwriting drifting downward is often a sign of tiredness, sadness, or possibly depression.

5 **Space between words and lines**
This represents the distance the writer places between him – or herself – and others. Thus, people who leave relatively little space between words require others' company – "They're needier, and possibly insecure," notes Widmer – while those who leave more space may be hard to get close to. Similarly, people who leave little space between lines need to get involved: "They tend to be big 'joiners,' and may get bogged down in the details of a situation," says Widmer. By contrast, writers who leave more space between lines are usually more independent and better at grasping the "big picture."

6 Besides space, graphologists also consider the zones writing is divided into: the upper (tall letters), middle (round letters), and lower (letters that extend downward). The balance among these three is very revealing. Here's what to look for:

7 The upper zone symbolizes one's mental and spiritual life; thus, someone whose handwriting features very tall letters tends to be an intellectual, "thinking" type. The middle zone, meanwhile, represents the everyday and how the person sees him or herself in relation to others. "People with a very large middle zone – rounded letters with little difference in height – are relatively self-centered and immature," says Widmer. "You often see this trait in teenagers' handwriting." Finally, the lower zone stands for one's physical side; athletes and other physical types often write with pronounced lower zones.

8 Widmer cautions that while these are generally accepted concepts of graphology, no single characteristic in writing is significant by itself. "It's not correct to say that crossing your T a certain way means something," he notes. "You have to look at handwriting in context."

A. The quick brown fox jumped over the lazy dogs

B. the quick brown fox jumped over the lazy dogs

C. the quick brown fox jumped over the lazy dogs.

Adapted from *Successful Meetings*.

## Before you read

**Look at the handwriting samples on the opposite page. What can you predict about each writer's personality? Write three characteristics for each sample.**

A. _____

B. _____

C. _____

## Reading

**Scan the text for words describing the writers of the above samples. Then read the whole text.**

## After you read

**A** **Find the words in *italics* in the reading. Then match each word with its meaning.**

__e__ 1. *deciphering* (par. 1)      a. making something known

____ 2. *tied to* (par. 3)      b. hold in your hand

____ 3. *needier* (par. 5)      c. very noticeable

____ 4. *get bogged down* (par. 5)      d. connected to

____ 5. *grasp* (par. 5)      e. making sense of

____ 6. *revealing* (par. 6)      f. wanting more from others

____ 7. *pronounced* (par. 7)      g. be unable to make progress

**B** **Look at the handwriting samples on the opposite page. Then answer the questions. Write *A*, *B*, or *C*.**

__A__ 1. Who probably does not like things to change?

____ 2. Who probably has few close friends?

____ 3. Who probably doesn't like to spend time alone?

____ 4. Who is probably a member of many organizations?

____ 5. Who probably doesn't worry about details?

____ 6. Who probably does silly things for his or her age?

**C** **Answer these questions.**

1. Would you pay for a professional handwriting analysis? Why or why not?
2. Do you think employers should use graphology to make hiring decisions? Why or why not?
3. Look at something you've written recently. According to the text, what does your handwriting say about your personality? Do you agree? Why or why not?

inking about
ersonal
xperience

canning

uessing
eaning from
ontext

nderstanding
etails

elating
ading to
ersonal
xperience

## Vocabulary expansion

Complete the crossword puzzle with words from the unit. (The words appear in the Preview. The numbers in parentheses after the clues below show the reading in which the word appears.)

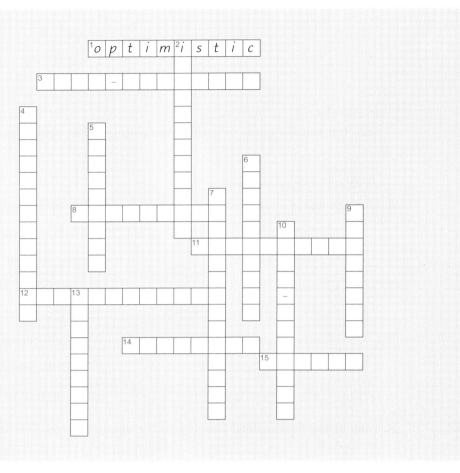

### Across

1. not pessimistic (3)
3. selfish (3)
8. preferring to be alone (2)
11. noisy and energetic (2)
12. can't be depended on (1)
14. friendly and not shy (2)
15. angry and unhappy (2)

### Down

2. thinking; academic (3)
4. very careful about work (1)
5. very shy and afraid (2)
6. ambitious, determined, and forceful (2)
7. not like most people (1)
9. unable to keep still; impatient (2)
10. confident (1)
13. gets excited easily (2)

## Personality and you

Look at the woman in the picture on page 66. Answer the questions.
Then compare answers with your classmates.

1. How open to new experience is she?
2. How agreeable is she?
3. How extroverted is she?

UNIT

# 10 Celebrity

You are going to read three texts about celebrity. First, answer the questions in the boxes.

**READING 1**

## I'm just another kid from Brooklyn

What is it like to be a celebrity? Find out what director Woody Allen says in this newspaper interview.

1. What movies has Woody Allen directed? Which have you seen?
2. What are the advantages of being a celebrity?
3. What are the disadvantages?

**READING 2**

## California law has paparazzi shuddering

This magazine article describes a law to stop photographers who follow California's celebrities.

1. Would you ever take a picture of a celebrity? Why or why not?
2. What publications feature photos of celebrities?
3. When do celebrities like being photographed? When do they dislike it?

**READING 3**

## Fan club confessions

In this magazine article, read the surprising results of a study on how celebrities influence the lives of their fans.

1. Have you ever collected posters or pictures of celebrities? If so, which ones?
2. Have you ever joined a fan club or visited a celebrity's website? If so, whose?
3. Which celebrities do you admire? Have you ever tried to imitate them?

## Vocabulary
**Find out the meanings of the words in *italics*. Then answer the questions.**

1. What celebrity's *autograph* would you like to have?
2. Which stars do celebrity *hounds* like to follow?
3. Who is a current *icon* in the music world?
4. Who is a popular teen *idol*?
5. Which celebrities don't like to be *in the public eye*?
6. Which celebrities have been *in the limelight* a lot recently?
7. Which celebrity is known for leading a very quiet life *offstage*?

# I'm just another kid from Brooklyn

1 Woody Allen is wearing a new hat as he steps from a rainy November afternoon into the Manhattan Film Center, where he edits all his new movies. He's dressed in autumnal colors, wools and corduroys and soft-soled Manhattan walking shoes, a pleasant smile lighting his eyes behind the trademark glasses.

2 **Celebrity is the second film you've made about America's fixation with fame and notoriety. (The first was Stardust Memories.) Why revisit the same theme?**

"Because I have been living a life involved with celebrity for many years, it's one of the things I do know about and can write about with some authority."

3 "Anyone can become a celebrity. And I have felt frustrated by my own celebrity. To me, and some other celebrities, there is a downside because we place a great value on privacy. Other celebrities have no problem with the limelight offstage, and love it. But I would be a complainer if I didn't admit the perks outweigh the downside. For me, it's no fun being in the public eye all the time but, being a New Yorker, I also get good tickets to the Knick games, seats for tough-to-get Broadway shows, restaurant reservations, and doctors on weekends. These are the positive things about being a celebrity, and they outweigh the annoyance of giving up your privacy."

4 **Is the public's obsession with celebrity greater than in the past?**

"It seems to be. When I did Stardust Memories years ago, the same guy in the movie who wanted my autograph and adored me ended up shooting me. About a month after my movie came out, John Lennon was shot in the same situation. Fans go crazy over celebrities. They adore them irrationally and love to see them get hurt. They really like that public flagellation of the celebrities they adore, but they still love the celebrity involved. It's a complex phenomenon, and the United States really lives in the cult of celebrity because they live in an opulent country and a lot of time and money for leisure. They have a thriving theater, television industry, film business, music, and painting. And sports is so enormous – as big as film, music, and theater put together. So the cult of celebrity is enormous here."

5 **When in Europe, did you feel hunted by celebrity hounds?**

"When I did my jazz tour there, I felt like a rock star. In every country on the tour they surrounded my hotel. It was an unreal experience. I don't live like that. I get up, exercise, walk the streets of Manhattan relatively unbothered, shop, and go to ball games, the theater, and restaurants. Perhaps in Europe, because I'm not over there that frequently, it's a big deal, and they express their demonstrative affection. And, hey, it's a big help for me in my movies, because if I didn't have that foreign support, my films wouldn't survive."

6 **Have the perks of your celebrity ever been outweighed by the downside?**

"I feel I'm a celebrity for better or worse. If I want the Knicks tickets and the good table at the restaurant, when a piece of gossip comes up, I'm willing to take it. I can't whine."

Adapted from *Daily News.*

edicting

## Before you read

**Look at the questions from the interview with Woody Allen. Then match each question with a part of his answers on the right.**

_____ 1. Why revisit the same theme?

_____ 2. Is the public's obsession with celebrity greater than in the past?

_____ 3. When in Europe, did you feel hunted by celebrity hounds?

_____ 4. Have the perks of your celebrity ever been outweighed by the downside?

a. In every country on the tour they surrounded my hotel.

b. It's one of the things I do know about and can write about . . .

c. If I want . . . the good table at the restaurant, I'm willing to take it.

d. Fans go crazy over celebrities. They adore them irrationally.

kimming

## Reading

**Skim the text to check your predictions. Then read the whole text.**

## After you read

uessing
eaning from
ontext

**A** **Find the words in _italics_ in the reading. Then match each word with its meaning.**

_h_ 1. *fixation* (par. 2)      a. disadvantage

_____ 2. *notoriety* (par. 2)      b. showing great wealth

_____ 3. *authority* (par. 2)      c. complain

_____ 4. *downside* (par. 3)      d. the state of being famous for something bad

_____ 5. *outweigh* (par. 3)      e. criticism as a punishment

_____ 6. *flagellation* (par. 4)      f. expert knowledge

_____ 7. *opulent* (par. 4)      g. be more important than

_____ 8. *whine* (par. 6)      h. act of always thinking about something

laking
statements

**B** **Check (✔) the statements you think Woody Allen would probably agree with.**

_____ 1. I love being in the limelight. There's nothing I don't love about it.

_____ 2. It's not fun when people want to know everything about my private life.

_____ 3. I never ask for special favors because I'm famous.

_____ 4. Being famous has its good and bad sides.

elating
ading to
ersonal
xperience

**C** **Answer these questions.**

1. Is it right for celebrities to use their fame to get special treatment? Why or why not?
2. Do you think the perks of celebrity outweigh the downside? Why or why not?
3. Would you like to be a celebrity? Why or why not?

# California law has paparazzi shuddering

1 They hide in trees, dangle from helicopters, even chase people down on motorcycles – all so that they can snap a shot of a celebrity. They are paparazzi – freelance photographers who make a living by taking pictures of the rich and famous.

2 This September, California, a state with plenty of celebrities, passed a law aimed at clamping down on paparazzi. The law prohibits photographers from trespassing on private property to take pictures, from using high-tech devices (such as telephoto lenses) to take pictures of people on private property, and from "persistently following or chasing someone in order to take a picture." Violators can be fined or spend time in jail. The United States Congress is considering passing a similar law.

3 Supporters of the California law say it will protect the privacy of celebrities, whom paparazzi have been bothering for years. Opponents say the law restricts photojournalists from doing their job.

### Stop snooping

4 Most celebrities seem to like having their pictures taken when they are in public at award shows or other events. After all, it's free publicity. But when they're not in public, they say, photographers should leave them alone. Yet paparazzi have been known to peek in windows and worse. Actor Michael J. Fox said that paparazzi have even "tried to pose as medical personnel at the hospital where [my wife] was giving birth to our son."

5 Celebrities have as much right to their privacy as anyone else, supporters of the law contend. Supporters further argue that the California law is a fair way to keep the press at bay, because the law still allows photographers to do their job. It only punishes them, supporters say, when they invade celebrities' privacy.

### The law is flawed

6 Opponents of the law say it violates the First Amendment to the United States Constitution, which guarantees that no laws will be made to limit "the freedom of speech, or of the press." Although some people might not consider paparazzi a part of the legitimate press, the California law does not single out paparazzi. It applies to photographers working for any publication.

7 Opponents of the law are also concerned about its wording. "Does 'persistently' mean following someone for six minutes, six seconds, or six days?" asked attorney Douglas Mirell. The wording of the law is too vague, critics complain, and could be used to punish almost any news photographer.

8 The United States needs a free press to keep the public informed about important issues, paparazzi law opponents say. Limiting the press in any way, they argue, limits the freedom of all.

9 Is California's law fair or unfair to photojournalists? Why?

Adapted from *Current Events*.

**READING TIP** Sometimes brackets [ ] are used to show corrections, explanations, or translations in someone else's speech or writing. For example, *my wife* (par. 4) probably replaces the name of Michael J. Fox's wife.

## Before you read

edicting

Look at the title and the picture on the opposite page. Then check (✔) the statement that you think best describes what the text will be about.

_____ 1. California has no laws to stop photographers from taking pictures of celebrities.

_____ 2. A new California law protects photographers from celebrities who don't want their pictures taken.

_____ 3. Support is mixed for a new California law to stop photographers from taking pictures of celebrities.

## Reading

:anning

Scan the text to check your prediction. Then read the whole text.

## After you read

nderstanding ain ideas

**A** Write the number of the paragraph or paragraphs next to each main idea.

_4_ a. This paragraph explains why celebrities think the law is necessary.
_____ b. This paragraph presents the supporters' and opponents' opinion of the law.
_____ c. This paragraph discusses why people support the law.
_____ d. These paragraphs discuss why people oppose the language used in the law.
_____ e. This paragraph describes various aspects of the law.
_____ f. This paragraph defines paparazzi.

uessing eaning from ontext

**B** Find the words in *italics* in the reading. Then match each word with its meaning.

_c_ 1. *clamp down* (par. 2)      a. charge money as a punishment

_____ 2. *trespass* (par. 2)      b. not clearly stated

_____ 3. *fine* (par. 2)      c. control

_____ 4. *single out* (par. 6)      d. choose for special treatment

_____ 5. *vague* (par. 7)      e. enter property without permission

istinguishing rguments

**C** Complete the chart.

| | Arguments against the law | Arguments in favor of the law |
|---|---|---|
| 1. | *restricts people from doing their job* | |
| 2. | | |
| 3. | | |

elating eading to ersonal xperience

**D** Answer these questions.

1. Why do you think the public is so interested in the lives of celebrities?
2. Do you think the California law is fair or unfair to photojournalists? Why?
3. Would you like to be a photojournalist? Why or why not?

# FAN CLUB CONFESSIONS

1 Collecting posters of Brad Pitt and scrapbooks about Princess Di may suggest more than empty celebrity crushes. While attachment to world-famous icons molds self-identity, a Canadian study found that starry-eyed 18-year-olds do not acknowledge their influence.

2 Professor of psychology Susan Boon and doctoral candidate Christine Lomore asked more than 200 Canadian undergraduates about their attachment to celebrities. The 79 students who expressed strong feelings toward an idol were then asked how seriously they took the relationship, and whether they had ever tried to emulate that person by dressing or behaving like them. They were also asked questions that ranged from how much time and money they had spent on their idol to how well they felt they knew the celebrity they admired. They answered questions on how much influence their idol had had on who they were and on how good they felt about themselves.

3 Participants indicated that despite strong attractions to their idols, they were not inspired to change their own behavior based on these celebrities' lives or accomplishments. Nor did they feel the media figures influenced their self-concept or feelings of self-worth.

4 Participants' responses to specific questions, however, told a very different story. Relatively few respondents reported that they had altered their physical appearance to appear more similar to their idols. However, one quarter indicated that they had made efforts to change aspects of their personality to bring it more in line with that of their favorite idol. Almost 60 percent admitted that an idol had influenced their attitudes and personal values, including their work ethic and views on morality. What's more, nearly half said that the celebrity inspired them to pursue activities in which their idol engaged – acting, music, sports – or to undertake a variety of pursuits such as creative writing or becoming a vegetarian.

5 Boon is not surprised by this inconsistency. "It's often hard to realize how much anyone influences us," she says. "We may also like to think that we develop our identity and sense of self rather than being influenced by others."

6 The majority of favorite idols listed by participants were movie stars and musicians. Actors from Cher to Tom Cruise topped the list, as did musicians such as Bono and Barbra Streisand. Interestingly, 85 percent of the celebrities cited were male. Boon attributes this finding to fewer female role models in categories like televised professional sports. In addition, "Men often choose other men as mentors and heroes, while women tend to select guys they are attracted to," she explains.

7 The list was peppered with icons who are dead, including John Wayne, Princess Diana and Albert Einstein. "Even if there's no possibility of interacting with an idol, celebrity attachments can still affect people's behavior and feelings about themselves," says Boon, who published the study in *Human Communication Research*. Parents perennially worry about teens' obsession with idols, but Boon notes that relatively few celebrities cited can be deemed negative influences. Most of the idols are well-respected idols in their fields – the kind of celebrities both young adults and their parents might easily admire. "Perhaps," concludes Boon, "the perception that celebrity attachments are harmful needs reexamining."

Adapted from *Psychology Today* and *Human Communication Research*.

sing previous
owledge

:anning

:cognizing
idience

iderstanding
:tails

elating
ading to
irsonal
:perience

## Before you read

**How much do you know about celebrities and their fans? Mark each statement true (*T*) or false (*F*).**

_____ 1. Fans always change their appearance to look more like their idols.

_____ 2. Fans never change aspects of their personality to be more like their idols.

_____ 3. Celebrities influence the attitudes and personal values of their admirers.

_____ 4. The celebrities most people admire are movie stars and musicians.

_____ 5. The celebrities most people admire are male.

_____ 6. Women tend to have female idols.

## Reading

**Scan the text to check your answers. Then read the whole text.**

## After you read

**A** **Who do you think the text was written for? Check (✔)the correct answer.**

_____ 1. members of celebrity fan clubs

_____ 2. executives in the entertainment industry

_____ 3. psychologists who conduct similar studies

_____ 4. people who are interested in psychology

**B** **Complete the chart with information about the study.**

| | |
|---|---|
| 1. Aim of the study: | *To determine whether attachment to celebrity affects people's behavior and feelings about themselves.* |
| 2. Number of participants in first part of the study: | |
| 3. Number of participants in second part of the study: | |
| 4. Sample questions participants answered in second part of the study: | |
| a. | |
| b. | |
| c. | |
| d. | |
| e. | |
| 5. Summary of the findings: | |

**C** **Answer these questions.**

1. Which celebrities in your country have the biggest influence on young people? How do these fans try to be like their idols?
2. Have you ever pursued an activity because of a celebrity? If so, what was it?
3. Has a celebrity ever influenced your attitudes or values? If so, how?

## Vocabulary expansion

**A** The prefix *out-* often means "better than or more than." For example, in Reading 1 *outweigh* means "more important than." Match each word with its meaning.

| | | | |
|---|---|---|---|
| _f_ | 1. *outdistance* | a. | be better or more successful than |
| | 2. *outdo* | b. | use intelligence to gain advantage over someone |
| | 3. *outgrow* | c. | be greater in number than (someone or something) |
| | 4. *outlast* | d. | sell more of or faster than another product |
| | 5. *outlive* | e. | run faster in order to escape or arrive before others |
| | 6. *outnumber* | f. | go faster or farther than, especially in a race |
| | 7. *outplay* | g. | continue to live after someone else has died |
| | 8. *outrun* | h. | win a game by using more skill than the other players |
| | 9. *outsell* | i. | become too large for something |
| | 10. *outsmart* | j. | continue to exist or work longer than something else |

**B** Complete each sentence with a verb from exercise A. Be sure to use the correct verb form.

1. The thief _____outsmarted_____ the police by changing his appearance.
2. Today, manufacturers are making smaller cars. They're cheaper, so they _____ larger cars.
3. Children usually _____ their parents.
4. The winning team completely _____ the other team.
5. My cousin is very competitive. He is always trying to _____ the rest of us.
6. The children needed new clothes because they _____ their clothes from last year.
7. If you see a fox, don't try to _____ it. Foxes move much faster than humans.
8. In this class, boys _____ girls. I think there are 20 boys and 10 girls.
9. James should be in the Olympics. Whenever he's in a race, he _____ the other runners.
10. These batteries are more expensive, but they should be good for a long time. They'll _____ the cheaper ones.

## Celebrity and you

Think of a celebrity you would like to interview. What area of the celebrity's life or work would you like to find out about? Write five questions to ask the celebrity. Then compare questions with your classmates.

# 11 The circus

You are going to read three texts about the circus. First, answer the questions in the boxes.

**READING 1**

## Getting serious about clowning

Read this newspaper article to find out what makes people want to become circus clowns.

1. Do you like clowns? Why or why not?
2. What qualities do you think a clown needs?
3. Why do you think some people want to become clowns?

**READING 2**

## Circus town

This newspaper article provides a glimpse into the lives of circus performers.

1. Have you ever been to the circus?
2. What circus acts do you like? Dislike?
3. What do you think a circus performer's life is like?

**READING 3**

## Tragedy at the circus; Circus safe for animals

Read two editorials on the issue of using animals in the circus.

1. Which animals typically perform in the circus?
2. Do you like circus acts involving animals? Why or why not?
3. What kinds of tragedies can take place at the circus?

### Vocabulary

**Find out the meanings of the words in the box. Then write each word under the correct heading.**

acrobat    aerialist    pantomime    slapstick    stilt-walking    animal trainer

**CIRCUS PERFORMERS**

_____

_____

_____

**CIRCUS ACTS**

_____

_____

_____

# Getting serious about clowning

1 The first batch of college acceptance letters goes into the mail next Friday. This means some anxious waiting for Gary Wheeler, although it's not one of the country's top colleges he has his sights set on. It's Clown College.

2 "I've got a positive attitude. I know I'm gonna make it," said Wheeler, one of 33 circus clown wannabes who auditioned for a spot at Ringling Bros. and Barnum & Bailey Clown College, a grueling two-month regimen of pratfalls and pantomime, slapstick and stilt-walking. Sound like fun?

3 John Deaton thinks so, which is why he's willing to fork over about $2,500 if he's accepted for the six-day-a-week, 14-hour-a-day summertime session. A 33-year-old massage therapist and storyteller, Deaton hoped to impress recruiters with the shiny red nose he kept pinched to his face throughout the two-hour audition. It's all part of the attraction of running off with the circus, which Deaton has wanted to do since he was 10. So if Clown College calls? "I'll drop and run. In a heartbeat. I'm on the bus, the plane, whatever."

4 "It's the world's biggest sandbox," agreed Brad Aldous, 25, a Clown College alum who now travels with Ringling. "It was very intense but it was a blast," he said of the rigorous course, required of all Ringling clowns.

5 Indeed, while many are called by the lure of the circus, only a few are chosen for Clown College. Each summer's class of 30 or so comes from more than 1,500 applicants who try out at sites

where the circus performs. The college lists 1,400 graduates, about a third of whom have signed clown contracts with Ringling.

6 The art of clowning has been traced back to 2270 B.C., when a nine-year-old Egyptian pharaoh recorded this critical appraisal: "A divine spirit – to rejoice and delight the heart." Clowns and circuses have continued to delight down through the centuries. In the United States, which hosted its first circus in 1793, assessment has been mixed. "It's an art form that people don't appreciate in this country," said Lavahn Hoh, a drama professor at the University of Virginia who also teaches at Clown College. Hoh raised a few eyebrows at the university several years ago when he proposed a class on circus history. The only course of its kind in the country, it is now in its fourteenth year and so popular that 150 students had to be

turned away one semester. Hoh, who caught the circus bug at age four, says it's where people can sit back "and forget about paying the mortgage and other worries."

7 That hasn't changed over the years, but clowns have, Hoh said, "A lot more college graduates are going into clowning. It's not just run-away-and-join-the-circus anymore." When she finishes college, sophomore Ashley Van Valkenburgh can't think of anything she'd rather be. "I've always wanted to go to Clown College," she said at her tryout. "Instead, I went to regular college." Paul Hood, 19, a freshman, said the circus is a natural for him since "I'm just a big kid at heart." He said he'd talked with his parents "and they're behind me all the way. It's just leaving one school for another school."

Adapted from *The Washington Post.*

edicting

canning

ecognizing
imilarity in
eaning

nderstanding
etails

elating
eading to
ersonal
xperience

## Before you read

**Look at the title and the picture on the opposite page. Then check (✔) what you think the text will be about.**

_____ 1. Clowns are trying to be more serious in their acts.

_____ 2. Circuses are trying to help clowns with their problems.

_____ 3. Training to become a clown is a serious business.

## Reading

**Scan the text to check your prediction. Then read the whole text.**

## After your read

**A** **Match each word or phrase with a word that is similar in meaning.**

_g_ 1. *have one's sights set on* (par. 1)          a. *fun* (par. 2)

_____ 2. *grueling* (par. 2)          b. *attraction* (par. 3)

_____ 3. *fork over* (par. 3)          c. *rigorous* (par. 4)

_____ 4. *audition* (par. 3)          d. *graduate* (par. 5)

_____ 5. *alum* (par. 4)          e. *assessment* (par. 6)

_____ 6. *a blast* (par. 4)          f. *pay* (par. 6)

_____ 7. *lure* (par. 5)          g. *want* (pars. 3, 7)

_____ 8. *appraisal* (par. 6)          h. *tryout* (par. 7)

**B** **Complete the brochure with words from the text.**

# CLOWN COLLEGE

**T**hink it's impossible to learn how to be a (1) ____*clown*____?
Think it takes years and years? At Clown College, we
teach all you need to know in classes that meet a total of
(2) _____ hours a week over a (3) _____ period.
Learn the art of (4) _____, (5) _____,
(6) _____, (7) _____, and much, much more.
Interested? Come in for an (8) _____ with our
recruiters. It'll take just (9) _____ hours of your
time and could change your life!

**C** **Answer these questions.**

1. Would you ever consider going to Clown College? Why or why not?
2. How do you think Clown College decides which applicants to accept?
3. What would your parents do if you told them you wanted to go to Clown College?

# Circus town

1  Somewhere in America on any given night exists a little town of 285 souls, all busily manufacturing delirium. Where, exactly, this town is located depends on Gaipo, general manager of the 131st Ringling Brothers and Barnum & Bailey Red Unit. Gaipo leads his people in many directions, and what a people they are: Brazilian dancers, Russian aerialists, Hungarian acrobats, Mexican stagehands and American clowns, plus an exotic assortment of tigers, zebras, elephants, camels, llamas, and horses.

2  As ancient lore would have it, the circus is a refuge for restless boys, freaks, and losers with violent pasts. In fact, aspiring entertainers don't run away with the circus – they audition. If they're lucky, they get two-year contracts, health insurance, and subsidized housing aboard the circus train. Gaipo is a college-educated company man, and the circus he presides over is a wholesome, if nomadic, enclave.

3  "We have everything you can imagine here," says Mark Oliver Gebel, the star animal trainer who followed in the footsteps of his father, Gunther Gebel-Williams. "We have our families, we have a school. I grew up here. It's been my whole life."

4  Growing up in the circus means dealing with extremes of both constancy and change. For Karen Stewart, the two-year-old daughter of the clown, Jay Stewart, each week brings a new lot in which to park the family's motor home, a new playground, library, and mall. But within that shifting landscape, Karen spends her days steeped in a communal warmth and comforting predictability that the village provides. Before a show, she marches through Clown Alley with a serious expression, inspecting the antics of her father's painted colleagues, whom she proudly calls "my clowns."

5  At 10 A.M. Thursday, as the arena filled with thousands of screaming children bused in from local schools, the circus' own children were in school backstage. Pam Boger, the head of the costume department, says of her 14-year-old daughter Whitney, "My daughter's in a very controlled environment, with a lot of people looking after her. I don't have to worry about drugs or anything else like that." (Boger's husband, Rick, does the camel and llama act.) With one teacher responsible for just five students, who range in age from 8 to 15, nobody gets left behind. If such constant scrutiny and scarce privacy might make an adolescent squirm even more than usual, Boger says that Whitney hasn't found out yet. "I don't think she really knows that she doesn't have her own space, because she's never experienced it. And she has friends: There's another girl in her class that she's close to, and also a boy."

6  Some of those children eventually will grow into their parents' – and their grandparents' – trades. While many of the performers are only passing through, some stay for life: Bello Nock, the show's high-risk comedic star, for instance, is a seventh-generation circus entertainer. Gebel, 31, acquired his seniority by upbringing, family tradition, and an uncanny bond with his beasts. "Some of these elephants have watched me grow up since I was a toddler," he explains. "And I've raised some of them from birth. Everybody in the circus is close. But this goes deeper."

7  Intimacy is an inescapable part of circus life. For the most part, the cast, crew, equipment, and animals all live on the train. Privilege is measured in an extra few square feet of space. Privacy is ensured by a thin partition. There is usually enough water onboard to go around, but not always. Still, nobody complains, at least not in public.

> **READING TIP**
> Always pay attention to words and phrases that show contrast – such as *in fact, but, while,* and *still.* They are important for understanding the meaning of a text. For example, *In fact* (par. 2) is used to introduce surprising information. *While* (par. 6) is used to illustrate an exception.

Adapted from *Newsday.*

inking
▪out
▪rsonal
▪perience

▪anning

▪essing
▪eaning from
▪ntext

▪derstanding
▪in ideas

▪lating
▪ading to
▪rsonal
▪perience

## Before you read

**Look at the title on the opposite page. Then check (✔) the statements about circus life that you think are true.**

_____ 1. Circus performers come from all over the world.

_____ 2. The circus was once a place for runaway boys and criminals.

_____ 3. Circus performers receive contracts, health insurance, and housing.

_____ 4. Children of circus performers don't go to school.

_____ 5. Many performers run away from their families to join the circus.

_____ 6. Performers and animals all live on a crowded circus train.

## Reading

**Scan the text to find out which statements above are true. Then read the whole text.**

## After you read

**A** **Find the words in the reading that match each definition.**

1. _____delirium_____ : feelings of excitement and happiness (par. 1)
2. _____ : traditional knowledge and stories (par. 2)
3. _____ : likely to benefit you physically, morally, or emotionally (par. 2)
4. _____ : belonging to or used by a group of people (par. 4)
5. _____ : amusing, silly, or strange behavior (par. 4)
6. _____ : show signs of embarrassment or discomfort (par. 5)
7. _____ : connection (par. 6)
8. _____ : something that separates a room (par. 7)

**B** **Circle the main idea of each paragraph.**

1. Paragraph 2: a. People in the circus are college-educated.
   (b.) The circus is for professionals.
2. Paragraph 3: a. Mark Oliver Gebel has lived with the circus all his life.
   b. Living with the circus is like living in a village.
3. Paragraph 4: a. For circus children, life is changeable but predictable.
   b. Each week the circus children's families move.
4. Paragraph 5: a. Circus children get more attention than other children.
   b. Circus children probably don't realize their lives are different.
5. Paragraph 6: a. Some children who grow up in the circus never leave.
   b. Circus children develop close bonds with the animals.
6. Paragraph 7: a. People who live on a circus train don't complain.
   b. Life on a circus train has some inconveniences.

**C** **Answer these questions.**

1. What information in the text surprised you about circus life?
2. What would you like about being a circus performer? What would you dislike?
3. Do you think the circus is a good place for a child to grow up? Why or why not?

# Tragedy at the circus

1 A rare tiger is dead and its trainer is gravely injured. It adds up to the worst nightmare for the circus that bills itself as the "Greatest Show on Earth." As the circus packed up and left, officials said the show would go on, even without the big cats that are one of the major attractions.

2 However, circus officials can't simply ignore the ethical issues they left behind. Even before this tragedy, the circus had become the focus of protests from animal rights activists. The protesters argue that tigers, elephants, and other wild animals are kept in cramped, artificial conditions and are forced to suffer for the profit of circus organizers.

3 The circus environment is at best an unnatural setting that places dangerous demands on animals and their trainers. At the very least, this incident should compel circus officials and outside authorities to take additional steps to assure that circus animals are treated humanely.

4 As humans have developed a greater understanding of endangered species and their dwindling habitats, greater efforts have to be made to place animals in captivity in the safest and most natural settings possible. Game preserves and modern zoos have moved away from treating wild animals as human entertainment. Given this heightened awareness, people have begun to view circus animal acts as unjustifiable. When enough would-be circus patrons come to that view, the acts will disappear, along with the risk of another such tragedy.

# Circus safe for animals

5 Our circus recently suffered one of the most tragic and devastating events in its history. While we appreciate the support and condolences from the community and the world, we are also taken aback by the opinion expressed by the editorial "Tragedy at the circus."

6 First, the animals that live and perform in the circus are not taken from the wild – this has been an international agreement for over 20 years.

7 Of even greater concern is the charge that we have somehow ignored the so-called ethical issues. We believe that humans and animals can – and should – live together in harmony.

8 We believe in the building of relationships between man and animal and in the important role of performing animals as messengers for their species.

9 We believe in our responsibility as caretakers of animals and protectors of their future.

10 We believe our circus is one of the only places left willing and able to support the unique role of performing animals in the future survival of the species.

11 Those who claim that circus life is unnatural and harmful to animals demonstrate ignorance and disregard for the facts. Life in the "wild" is not secure, but a constant struggle for survival as the world's human population grows. To ignore these realities is the greatest crime against the animal kingdom.

12 In its 200-year history, the circus in the United States has shown the world that humans and animals can live together. Perhaps even more relevant is the role the circus plays in reminding us of our responsibility to the animal kingdom, the conservation of species, habitat preservation, and our responsibility as animal caretakers.

13 This circus has proven that the range of animal intelligence and physical ability is greater than what we assumed. Within the circus community, animals and humans live together in harmony, people are educated, and species saved.

Adapted from the *St. Petersburg Times.*

## Before you read

**Look at the titles and picture on the opposite page. The first title is from a newspaper editorial, and the second is the circus's response to the editorial. Then answer the questions below.**

1. What do you think the tragedy was?
2. What opinion do you think the editorial expressed?
3. How do you think the circus responded?

## Reading

**Scan the text to check your predictions. Then read the whole text.**

## After you read

**A** **Find the complete sentences in the text. Then write fact (*F*) or opinion (*0*).**

   *F*   1. As the circus packed up . . . major attractions. (par. 1)

        2. However, circus officials . . . ethical issues they left behind. (par. 2)

        3. Even before this tragedy . . . protests from animal rights activists. (par. 2)

        4. First, the animals . . . international agreement for over 20 years. (par. 6)

        5. We believe that humans and animals . . . live together in harmony. (par. 7)

        6. Those who claim that . . . ignorance and disregard for the facts. (par. 11)

**B** **Circle the statements that express the circus's response to each argument in the editorial.**

1. The circus ignores ethical issues.
   a. The circus believes animals and humans should live together in harmony.
   b. The writer of the editorial is ignoring the ethical issues.
   c. The recent event at the circus was tragic.
2. Wild animals are kept in cramped, artificial conditions.
   a. The circus shows the world that humans and animals can live together.
   b. The circus is responsible for protecting the conditions in which the animals live.
   c. Animals that live and perform in the circus are not taken from the wild.
3. The circus is an unnatural setting that places dangerous demands on animals.
   a. Nothing the animals do in the circus is dangerous.
   b. Circuses prove that animal intelligence is greater than we assumed.
   c. Life in the "wild" is not secure, but a constant struggle for survival.

**C** **Answer these questions.**

1. Do you think animals should perform for human entertainment? Why or why not?
2. Do you think circuses protect endangered species? If so, how?
3. What steps would assure that circus animals are treated humanely?

## Vocabulary expansion

**A** Find the phrasal verbs below in this unit's readings. Then write the letter of the correct definition next to each phrasal verb. (Be careful! There are two extra answers.)

_f_  1. *fork over* (reading 1, par. 3)

___  2. *try out* (reading 1, par. 5)

___  3. *turned away* (reading 1, par. 6)

___  4. *sit back* (reading 1, par. 6)

___  5. *run away* (reading 2, par. 2)

___  6. *looking after* (reading 2, par. 5)

___  7. *passing through* (reading 2, par.6)

___  8. *go on* (reading 3, par. 1)

a. rest in a comfortable position
b. to make an attempt to do something
c. sit and eat something
d. taking care of
e. escape
f. spend
g. continue
h. not allowed into a place
i. staying for a short time
j. compete for a position or job

**B** Complete the poster with phrasal verbs from exercise A.

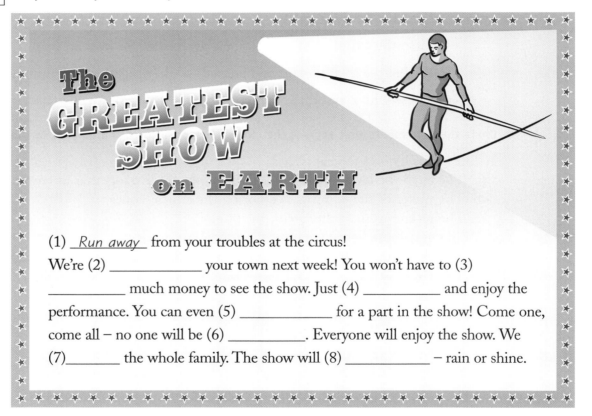

★ The **GREATEST SHOW** on **EARTH** ★

(1) _Run away_ from your troubles at the circus!

We're (2) _____ your town next week! You won't have to (3) _____ much money to see the show. Just (4) _____ and enjoy the performance. You can even (5) _____ for a part in the show! Come one, come all – no one will be (6) _____. Everyone will enjoy the show. We (7)_____ the whole family. The show will (8) _____ – rain or shine.

## The circus and you

Hold a debate on whether animals should be allowed to perform in the circus. Separate into two groups. One group will argue for allowing animal performances, and the other group will argue against them. Before the debate, conduct research that supports your group's argument.

UNIT

# 12 Martial arts

You are going to read three texts about martial arts. First, answer the questions in the boxes.

READING 1

## Shaolin Temple

Read this newspaper article to learn about the home of Asian martial arts.

1. What forms of martial arts are practiced in your country?
2. What do you know about the history of martial arts?
3. Do you meditate? If so, how?

READING 2

## The karate generation

Find out why karate has become so popular with young Americans in this magazine article.

1. When do you think people start learning martial arts?
2. Why do you think people study martial arts?
3. What are the benefits of karate?

READING 3

## Iron and Silk

This excerpt from a memoir tells how a young man's martial art skills help him get out of trouble.

1. Do you like to watch martial arts demonstrations?
2. Are martial arts experts in your country respected? Why or why not?
3. What kinds of weapons are used in martial arts?

## Vocabulary

**Find out the meanings of the words in *italics*. Check (✔) the statements that you think are true.**

_____ 1. Karate helps develop *agility* and self-confidence.

_____ 2. Kids think that learning karate improves their *cognitive* skills.

_____ 3. Practicing martial arts strengthens your *limbs*.

_____ 4. Some highly stylized martial arts *routines* look strange.

_____ 5. Some forms of meditation involve *slugging* and *slashing* with a sword.

_____ 6. Martial arts moves include *swiping* an arm or *thrusting* a foot into the air.

# Shaolin Temple

1   As you stroll through the Shaolin Monastery complex, you are apt to be startled when a teenage boy in a sweatsuit suddenly thrusts a foot into the sky, or another practices the fine art of hanging from a tree by his toes.

2   This cluster of wooden buildings at the foot of Song Mountain in central China is the home of Zen Buddhism and of Asian martial arts. The unexpected movements represent typical horseplay of students from the school on the hill behind the monastery. The students might be practicing from among the thousands of special martial moves taught here – one called "flowers hidden among the leaves," in which a leg seems to come out of nowhere or "sweeping an army of thousands," a powerful swipe with a staff intended to mow down multiple attackers.

3   If you think that gentle Buddhism seems incompatible with the violent dispatch of opponents by kicking, slugging, or slashing with a sword, then you do not really understand meditation, De Yang says.

4   At 32, De Yang is an acclaimed master of the monastery's stylized and sometimes bizarre routines of strength and self-defense. He is also one of the senior monks, practicing the form of meditation known in China as Chan and in Japan and the West as Zen.

5   "Chan and martial arts are one," he says. The practice of martial routines is simply a physical expression of Chan, the meditation exercises used in the pursuit of spiritual enlightenment.

6   Visitors who search for easy truths here, whether about the meaning of Chan or of a monastery that has become a

major tourist attraction, are bound to be disappointed. What is indisputably true is that the monastery is thriving, benefiting from a kung-fu-movie-driven fascination with martial arts and a surge in domestic tourism.

7   Two to three million people visit the Shaolin Monastery each year, enjoying the elegant grounds and buildings filled with old inscriptions, fading murals, and reputed artifacts of the monastery's fabled history. They also watch exhibitions of martial arts routines and see monks break bricks or other hard objects with their heads.

8   The crowds and shows destroy the serenity and have led to charges of commercialism, but they also bring in money for restoring buildings that were repeatedly vandalized through the centuries. In the valley surrounding Shaolin, a whole town of shops and dozens of competing martial arts schools has sprung up.

9   The monastery itself houses 78 monks, not all of them martial arts

masters. Its school has 400 students, from elementary through high school. Only about 20 are girls. The younger students learn reading and math, but their main purpose is to become accomplished in martial arts. Some dream of becoming fighting monks themselves.

10   The romance of Shaolin rests on legends that are too good to question. It is said that in the sixth century A.D. an Indian Buddhist missionary called Bodhidharma arrived. He climbed into a cave and sat in intense meditation for nine years. He was so persevering that his shadow became permanently imprinted on the cave wall, and today that piece of rock, chipped out, is a prime sight in the monastery.

11   Bodhidharma founded the Chan sect and also, while trying to limber up his cramped limbs during those years of sitting, practiced exercises that would develop into Shaolin martial arts.

Adapted from *The New York Times*.

**READING TIP**   Writers often use appositives to give a definition or explanation, especially when the word has a foreign origin. For example, the writer explains *Chan* (par. 5) as *the meditation exercises used in the pursuit of spiritual enlightenment.*

## Before you read

**Look at the picture on the opposite page and the words and phrases below.**
**Then check (✔) those you think you will read in the text.**

_____ 1. *home of Zen Buddhism*          _____ 4. *sports psychologist*

_____ 2. *soccer, basketball, and baseball*     _____ 5. *break bricks*

_____ 3. *spiritual enlightenment*         _____ 6. *commercialism*

## Reading

**Scan the text to check your predictions. Then read the whole text.**

## After you read

**A** **Find the words in *italics* in the reading. Then match each word with its meaning.**

__c__ 1. *startled* (par. 1)          a. unable to exist together

_____ 2. *horseplay* (par. 2)        b. paintings on a wall

_____ 3. *incompatible* (par. 3)      c. surprised

_____ 4. *dispatch* (par. 3)        d. intentionally damaged

_____ 5. *murals* (par. 7)          e. rough, noisy behavior

_____ 6. *vandalized* (par. 8)       f. sending away

**B** **Answer the questions.**

1. Why are both martial arts and meditation practiced at Shaolin Monastery?
2. Why do tourists visit the monastery?
3. Why do children come to stay there?
4. Why do people visit the cave wall nearby?

**C** **The following paragraphs appeared in the original article. Write the number of the paragraph they should follow.**

_____ a. Bai Long, 16, from Inner Mongolia, grew up idolizing the Shaolin fighters. He moved here two years ago and hopes to become a disciple of De Yang, then eventually to take vows as a monk. "It's my ideal," he said, blushing.

_____ b. Just how stretching was transformed into warrior routines seems to be in some dispute. By some accounts, the monks honed their skills to rob from the rich and give to the poor. By others, the monks, as some of the richest people around, had to learn to defend themselves from bandits.

**D** **Answer these questions.**

1. Do you think of martial arts as an art, a sport, a method of self-defense, or a way of life? Why?
2. Do you think tourism is good for the monastery? Why or why not?
3. Do you believe physical exercise can enlighten you? Why or why not?

# The KARATE generation

1 Vincent Almeroth tried gymnastics. He tried soccer, basketball, and baseball too. But the 11-year-old has dyslexia, which made it difficult for him to focus on the playing field. There was too much unanticipated movement and interaction with other kids, says his mother, Lisa Terranova. Then three years ago Vincent tried karate. It was an instant hit. His agility and self-confidence improved almost immediately, and his reading has progressed as well. Now he is a blue belt. Karate has "given him a greater ability to focus and to struggle with things that are difficult," says Terranova. Vincent puts it more simply: "Karate makes me feel strong and good and happy."

2 Vincent is one of a growing number of kids who are finding success through karate. In fact, the number of martial arts students under 12 has grown 15 percent a year for the past five years, says Katherine Thiry of the National Karate-do Federation. "Martial arts is everywhere – rec centers, churches, the inner city, and suburbs," says Joe Corley, who founded a chain of karate schools.

3 For kids, the appeal lies in the sport's tangible rewards: different colored belts and respect on the playground. Those things are especially meaningful to children who are on the social fringe, unaccustomed to athletic achievement or who may be the targets of bullies. Karate – literally "empty hand" in Japanese – and its cousins judo, jujitsu, and tae kwon do develop strength and coordination while teaching children how to avoid conflict and defend themselves if attacked. Its individualistic bent is especially attractive to the children who are regularly picked last for the soccer team. "In soccer, unless children have a modicum of talent, they're relegated to the sidelines," says Thiry. "[In karate], even the most uncoordinated, unfocused person can achieve."

4 Parents often notice a rise in their children's self-esteem when they start karate. And with good reason: A study by Bob Schleser, a sports psychologist, found that children between 7 and 18 who took karate dramatically increased their "perceived competence" in areas ranging from social and cognitive skills to maternal acceptance. "Karate gives a general sense of confidence and personal control," says Schleser.

5 That's especially beneficial to children with learning or developmental disabilities. At the martial arts academy where Vincent studies, nearly half of director Jeff Kohn's 110 students have special needs. For six-year-old James Fuller, who has spina bifida, karate has "really changed his life," says his mom, Joanne. Because of his disorder, James has to wear braces and shoes rather than go barefoot. But the experience has helped him learn to cope with his disability.

6 Parents agree that the exact nature of the training is less important than the quality of the teacher. "You shouldn't be too concerned with the [martial arts] style but with how the instructor works with children," says Rob Colasanti, vice president of the National Association of Professional Martial Artists. Good karate instructors – though they might be strict – should also offer plenty of praise and encouragement, he says.

7 Indeed, Lisa Terranova is quick to credit Kohn for her son's achievement. Vincent has made so much academic progress that he is being moved from a special school for learning-disabled kids to a regular school.

Adapted from *Newsweek*.

## Before you read

Check (✔) the statements you agree with.

_____ 1. Kids who aren't athletic can be good at martial arts.

_____ 2. Bullies don't bother kids who practice martial arts.

_____ 3. As martial arts become popular, more kids are practicing meditation.

_____ 4. Martial arts teach kids how to avoid conflict and defend themselves.

_____ 5. Even uncoordinated, unfocused people can succeed in karate.

_____ 6. People with physical disabilities can't do martial arts.

## Reading

Scan the text to find out which statements above are true. Then read the whole text.

## After you read

**A** Write the number of each paragraph next to its main idea.

__4__ a. Karate helps improve children's self-esteem.

_____ b. The teacher is very important in martial arts training.

_____ c. More and more children are taking martial arts classes.

_____ d. All children can succeed at karate.

_____ e. Karate can help children become better students.

_____ f. Karate benefits children in many ways.

_____ g. Karate can help children who have special problems.

**B** Find the words and phrases in the reading that match these definitions. Write one word on each line.

1. difficulty with reading and writing        _dyslexia_ (par. 1)

2. started an organization        _____ (par. 2)

3. achievements that can be touched or felt        _____ _____ (par. 3)

4. not accepted by many people        _____ _____ _____ (par. 3)

5. not participating actively, as in a game        _____ _____ _____ (par. 3)

6. what people think they're good at        _____ _____ (par. 4)

**C** Answer these questions.

1. Do you think it's better to learn martial arts as a child or as an adult? Why?
2. Do young people in your country find martial arts appealing? Why or why not?
3. What are the less "tangible rewards" that children get from sports?

elating to the
pic

canning

nderstanding
ain ideas

uessing
eaning from
ontext

elating
eading to
ersonal
xperience

# Iron and Silk

1     For some reason I always had bad luck in Canton. In August 1984, on my way out of China after two years in Hunan Province, I was delayed at the Canton train station for half a day because of the seven-foot leather bag I carried. It contained five swords, four sabers, a staff, two hooked swords, and some knives. I had receipts and photos and a manila folder full of Foreign Affairs Bureau correspondence to prove that the weapons were all either gifts from my teachers or had been purchased in local stores, that none of them was an antique, and that I was the legitimate student of a well-known martial artist residing in Hunan, but the officials right away saw an opportunity to play their favorite game, Let's Make a Regulation.

2     "This bag is too long. You can't take it on the train. There's a regulation." We discussed this point for a while, and eventually the regulation was waived. "But these weapons are Chinese cultural artifacts. They cannot leave China, that's a regulation. You can take the bag, though." In time it was determined that the weapons might conceivably leave China, but I would need special permission from a certain office which would require a certain period of time to secure, so wouldn't I stay in Canton for a few days and come back with the proper documentation? My flight from Hong Kong to New York left in two days; I was desperate not to miss it. As I walked around the train station trying to think up a new strategy, I happened to bump into a Cantonese policeman I had met a year before. When I told him my problem he took me by the arm and led me back to the train station, where he began arguing on my behalf. He talked with the officials for over an hour about this and that, occasionally touching on the subject of my bag and its contents, then gently retreating to other matters. He eventually suggested that I give a short martial arts demonstration there in the train station – "Wouldn't that be fun?" He asked the people sitting on the long wooden benches in the station to make room for a performance, then helped them move the benches out of the way. I warmed up for a few minutes, took off my shoes, and began a routine. Somewhere in mid-air, my pants split wide open in the back. A crowd of giggling ladies rushed forward with needles and thread ready, followed by an equal number of old men with incurable illnesses who believed that I must have learned traditional medicine as part of my martial arts training, convincing the officials to let me through without further delay. The policeman helped me get on the train, then sat with me until it began to move. He hopped off, wished me well, then saluted as the train left the station.

Adapted from *Iron and Silk*.

## Before you read

Look at the picture on the opposite page and these phrases from the text.
What do you think happens in the story?

> delayed at the Canton train station  proper documentation
> five swords, four sabers  give a short martial arts demonstration
> student of a well-known martial artist  my pants split

## Reading

Scan the text to check your prediction. Then read the whole text.

## After you read

**A** The text is from a book. What do you think the book is about?
Check (✔) the correct answer.

_____ 1. how to travel by train in China

_____ 2. the rise of a powerful martial arts master

_____ 3. an American's experiences living in China

**B** Find and correct the eight mistakes in the following report. (Note: The first mistake has been corrected.)

A young American at the train station wanted to ~~enter~~ *leave* China with weapons he had

illegally purchased. He was told the only way for him to leave was to go back to Hunan

and return with the proper documentation. A couple of days later, he came back with a

policeman from Hunan. This policeman gave a martial arts demonstration. The

policeman finally convinced the officials to let him get on the train without the weapons.

**C** Check (✔) the statements that are true.

_____ 1. The writer speaks Chinese.

_____ 2. The writer didn't think anybody would question him about his weapons.

_____ 3. The writer respects officials in China.

_____ 4. The writer had been in Canton the year before.

_____ 5. The people at the train station didn't want to watch an American.

_____ 6. Martial arts training in China includes learning how to treat illnesses.

**D** Answer these questions.

1. Is there any place where you've always had bad luck? If so, where?
2. Have you ever been stopped and questioned by a travel official? If so, what happened?
3. What aspect(s) of your culture would be difficult for a foreigner to master or
   understand?

## Vocabulary expansion

**A** Read the definitions. Then write the second half of each hyphenated word. Use the words in the box.

| | | | | |
|---|---|---|---|---|
| control | importance | image | interest | portrait |
| discipline | reliance | improvement | pity | taught |

1. **self-** *reliance*   *n*  depending on yourself rather than other people
2. **self-** _____   *n*  sadness about your own problems
3. **self-** _____   *n*  learned without a teacher or trainer
4. **self-** _____   *n*  making yourself a better-skilled person
5. **self-** _____   *n*  power over your emotions and actions when upset or excited
6. **self-** _____   *n*  the ability to do things that you don't want to do
7. **self-** _____   *n*  a picture you paint of yourself
8. **self-** _____   *n*  the belief that you are more valuable than other people
9. **self-** _____   *n*  thinking of what is best for yourself rather than for others
10. **self-** _____   *n*  your opinion of how you appear to other people

**B** Write the words in exercise A in the correct column. Then add three other nouns that begin with *self-*.

| Positive meaning | Negative meaning | Neutral meaning |
|---|---|---|
| self-reliance | | |
| | | |
| | | |
| | | |
| | | |
| | | |

## Martial arts and you

Work in small groups. Do a survey of people's interest in martial arts. First, come up with five questions.

Example: *Do you practice any form of martial arts?*

*Do you like movies that feature martial arts?*

Then ask five classmates, friends, or family members. Report your findings to the class.

UNIT

# 13 Fashion

You are going to read three texts about fashion. First, answer the questions in the boxes.

**READING 1**

## Smart clothes

Read about technological innovations in clothing in this article from a website.

1. How do you think technology will change the clothing of the future?
2. Do you have a laptop or PDA? If so, how do you carry it?
3. How do you think computer chips could be used in clothing?

**READING 2**

## It's a dog's life

This Japanese newspaper article explores the role of dogs in today's fashion world.

1. Do you have a dog? If so, what have you bought for it recently?
2. What things do people usually buy for their pets?
3. What kinds of things do dogs like? Are they expensive?

**READING 3**

## How to separate trends from fads

This magazine article explains why some products and services disappear quickly while others last for years.

1. What things are popular now? How long have they been popular?
2. Do you wear clothes similar to those worn by the mainstream?
3. What new products have taken off? Would you buy any of them?

## Vocabulary

**Find out the meanings of the words in *italics*. Then answer the questions.**

1. How much attention do you pay to *accessories*?
2. Who are the *best-dressed* people you know?
3. What *attire* do you wear on special occasions?
4. What styles do you think are *avant-garde*?
5. Are jeans an *indispensable* part of your wardrobe?
6. Are your parents' ideas about fashion *in sync* or *out of sync* with your ideas?
7. Do you pay attention to what the *trendsetters* are wearing?
8. Do you think that you are *trendy*?

# Smart clothes

1 You may soon see some truly avant-garde fashions on the street, but you won't find them in *Vogue* or *GQ*. "Smart clothes" — attire containing portable computers, sensors, and wireless transmitters — will definitely not get you on *People* magazine's best-dressed list. But it may get you out from behind your desk.

2 Wearable computers represent one of the latest technological advancements. Surgical circuit implants – enabling image processing, rapid data retrieval and storage, wireless communication, and environmental sensor feedback – aren't technically possible yet. However, people can still wear their computers as attire. Laptops and PDAs have allowed people to take their computers on the road, but they still have to stop whatever they're doing to use them. Wearable computers, in contrast, are designed to always be on, always sensing the environment, ready to tell the "wearer" about incoming data as necessary. Also, the equipment is generally hands-free.

3 A typical set of smart clothes might include:
- A CPU with hard-disk, worn in a backpack or waist pocket.
- A wireless modem.
- A display worn over one eye that allows the wearer to view real and virtual worlds simultaneously. For instance, one device uses LCDs (liquid crystal displays) and mirrors to display a full-screen-sized image. There are also eyeglasses that superimpose data on top of the lens.
- One-handed input devices such as keyboards or joysticks. One, for example, forms characters with a combination of twelve finger buttons. It includes a tilt sensor that imitates a computer mouse.
- A head-mounted camera.

4 Additional accessories might include a wireless fax machine, a GPS (global positioning system) transmitter, a microphone, and an environmental sensor for temperature and air quality readings.

5 It's likely that wearable computers and their accessories will soon be smoothly integrated into normal-looking clothing, but for now these styles are definitely awkward and bizarre.

6 This doesn't seem to bother fans, who talk about advantages such as data-on-demand from a hard disk or the Web, the ability to read and send e-mail while walking (safely) down the street, or the convenience of viewing a manual (hands-free) while repairing a motorcycle. According to the *Boston Globe*, one creative user replaced his apartment thermostat with a radio receiver that picks up signals from sensors in his clothes. When he's cold, the heater automatically comes on.

7 Smart clothing is a high-interest area. The first International Symposium on Wearable Computers drew academic and industry researchers, vendors and research sponsors. Considering all the interest they have been generating, the future looks bright for smart clothes.

> **READING TIP**
> Acronyms are created from the first letter of each word in a series. Writers use them because they are shorter than the words they replace. For example, a *PDA* (par. 2) is a "personal digital assistant." Also, *CPU* (par. 3) is the acronym for "central processing unit."

Adapted from *Networker*.

## Before you read

Check (✔) the features you think the clothing of the future will have.

_____ 1. portable computers

_____ 2. wireless fax machines

_____ 3. environmental sensors

_____ 4. cameras

_____ 5. microphones

_____ 6. compact disc players

## Reading

Scan the text to find out which clothing above the writer mentions. Then read the whole text.

## After you read

**A** Find the words in *italics* in the reading. Circle the meaning of each word.

1. If something *gets you out from* somewhere, it **helps you escape / helps you understand / helps you find** it. (par. 1)
2. Something that *enables* something else **makes it difficult / makes it impossible / makes it possible**. (par. 2)
3. If equipment is *hands-free*, you **don't have to pay for / don't have to touch / don't need special skill to use** it. (par. 2)
4. If you do things *simultaneously*, you do them **with difficulty / at the same time / fashionably**. (par. 3)
5. If something is *awkward*, it is **uncomfortable / fashionable / innovative**. (par. 5)
6. *Data-on-demand* is **information that is hard to understand / very specific information / information when you want it**. (par. 6)

**B** Complete the meaning of each pair of sentences. Write same (*S*) or different (*D*).

_____ 1. Surgical circuit implants aren't technically possible yet.
We do not currently have the technology for surgical circuit implants.

_____ 2. Laptops and PDAs have allowed people to take their computers on the road.
People can use laptops and PDAs to do computer work when they travel.

_____ 3. Wearable computers, in contrast, are designed to be always on.
People who have wearable computers must always wear them.

_____ 4. It's likely that wearable computers and their accessories will soon be smoothly integrated into normal-looking clothes.
Wearable computers and accessories will probably soon be a part of regular clothing.

**C** Answer these questions.

1. In what ways are wearable computers practical? If what ways are they impractical?
2. Would you want to wear smart clothes? Why or why not?
3. Do you think wearable computers will be popular in the future? Why or why not?

# It's a dog's life

1 It seems that ever since fashion models in Japan started revealing their love for their dogs in magazines and on television, the meaning of "man's best friend" has taken a new turn. Dogs have become an almost indispensable accessory for young people trying to lead a trendy life. One women's magazine even wrote in a recent issue featuring dog accessories: "The cute combination of a collar and a silver necklace is something we must imitate!"

2 Dog lovers have long considered their canine counterparts as equals, but recent trends show that, at times, dogs are more equal than humans. Raincoats and sweaters for dogs, pet hotels, and colorful collars are nothing new. But the notable feature among dogs in Japan, as is the case with their human counterparts, is the brand craze. The Hermes' O'Kelly collar, from which dangles a lock similar to the ones found on the brand's famous Kelly handbags, is one of the most sought-after items. Burberry's checked raincoat would go nicely with young girls sporting Burberry skirts and scarves. Kate Spade's dog carriers are just as expensive as the popular designer's colorful tote bags; and Gucci's dog Frisbees have proven so popular, they are now out of stock.

3 We have more in common with our canine friends than just luxury goods, though. Many people take their dogs' mental and physical well-being seriously, and manufacturers have been ready to meet this new demand. A magnetized collar that is said to increase a dog's circulation, stimulate the appetite and

metabolism, and ease stress and fatigue is now on sale. There are also fragrances, bath salts, and aromatherapy shampoos for dogs, while public baths – or sinks, rather – and aromatherapy salons that are exclusively for dogs are opening up around Tokyo. Classes offered by community centers that teach owners how to cook and knit for their dogs also have been gaining attention recently.

4 Toy manufacturer Takara Co., in February, will market Bowlingual, a gadget that recognizes, analyzes, and categorizes a dog's voice according to "levels of emotion." Consisting of a tiny microphone that hangs around the neck of the animal and a Tamagotchi-like display that can be monitored, the device allows owners to identify how their dog is feeling from a selection of six different emotions.

5 Mayumi Yokoyama, director of a Japanese branch of United States-based Three Dog Bakery, says attitudes toward dogs have definitely changed in the past decade or so. Biscuits and cakes from the bakery are all made from vegetable-based ingredients, and are free of salt, sugar, preservatives, and chemical substances. The Japanese branch opened its doors three months ago in Daikanyama, Tokyo, where many wealthy, fashionable people live with their dogs. To help meet the needs of these people, an increasing number of cafes and restaurants in the area have been allowing dogs onto their premises.

6 "People used to think that dogs should be kept outside, but today many look at them as part of their families, or even partners," Yokoyama said. The delicacies available at the bakery all look exquisite even by human standards – take for instance, the decorated cakes for special occasions – befitting the status of a human's "partner."

Adapted from *The Daily Yomiuri*.

## Before you read

Who uses these things? Mark each item dogs (*D*), people (*P*), or both (*B*).

_____ 1. raincoats          _____ 5. frisbees

_____ 2. sweaters          _____ 6. fragrances

_____ 3. hotels            _____ 7. shampoo

_____ 4. collars           _____ 8. cakes

## Reading

Scan the text to check your answers. Then read the whole text.

## After you read

**A** Find and underline the answers to these questions in the text.

1. When did the meaning of man's best friend change? (par. 1, 18 words)
2. What is the notable feature among dogs in Japan? (par. 2, 3 words)
3. What is one of the most desired items? (par. 2, 4 words)
4. What hangs from the Hermes' O'Kelly collar? (par. 2, 13 words)
5. What is now on sale? (par. 3, 3 words)
6. What two places for dogs are opening up around Tokyo? (par. 3, 2 words; par. 3, 2 words)
7. What does Bowlingual consist of? (par. 4, 19 words)
8. What delicacies are sold at the bakery? (par. 6, 5 words)

**B** Write the products from the text that this dog should use.

My owner wants me to match her Kelly bag.
3. _____

I don't smell very nice.
2. _____

I have bad circulation.
1. *magnetized collar*

My owner wants to know my moods.
4. _____

I shouldn't have any sugar.
5. _____

My birthday is next week.
6. _____

**C** Answer these questions.

1. Do people in your country have dogs as pets? If so, how do they treat them?
2. Would you buy any of the products in the text for a dog? If so, which ones?
3. Do you think it's a good idea for owners to buy luxury items for their pets? Which of the products do you think are most wasteful?

# How to separate trends from fads

1 Marketers always want to know whether a new development is going to be a trend or a fad. By definition, a trend lasts at least five years, is broadly based, and represents significant marketing opportunities. A fad, on the other hand, has a much shorter life cycle, is usually confined to one or two industries, and represents limited potential. Naturally, marketers want to cash in on trends but avoid getting burned by fads. Here is a three-step checklist to help determine whether a new development will be a trend or a fad.

## A. What is driving it?

2 A trend has a solid foundation that supports its growth – demographics, values, lifestyle, and technology. A fad does not have such a solid foundation, but is usually driven by pop culture, fashion, "the trendy crowd," and media.

3 Casual attire, for example, is a trend driven by demographics (a heavier population that prefers looser clothing), shifting values (comfort takes precedence over fashion), and lifestyle (informality in the home and workplace).

## B. How accessible is it to the mainstream?

4 Analyze the mainstream today to determine how much it will have to change to adopt a new development. This adjustment process can take five years or more before the mainstream is "ready." To evaluate accessibility, consider the following:

5 **Appeal** Buying books online is becoming a way of life for many Americans because the purchase decision is usually made in advance and seldom requires examination of the actual product. Most people are willing to wait a few days for delivery because books are usually a non-essential purchase. Buying groceries online, however, is not going to take off because it is out of sync with the way people shop for groceries. Food is an "essential" purchase that is seldom done in advance, as few people can wait for delivery and there is often no one at home to receive deliveries.

6 **Ease of adoption** Products will be more accessible if they do not require a change in behavior or tastes, are simple to use, and do not involve an educational process. Once the price of CD players came down, the mainstream quickly converted to this format because it was superior to tapes and LPs, and just as easy to use.

7 **Price** Some developments may have mainstream appeal, but will remain marginal because people are either unwilling to pay a premium price for it (environmentally safe dry cleaning) or simply unable to afford it (European luxury cars).

8 **Availability** Many people would like to surf or snowboard, for example, but participation will remain limited due to each sport's geographical requirements: You need the ocean for surfing, the mountains for snowboarding.

## C. Is it broadly based?

9 If you can find related examples of a new development in different categories or industries, it is likely to be a trend. Eastern influences, for example, are permeating our culture – in spirituality, healthcare, food, fitness, design, and pop culture – so this is a trend. Belgian influences, on the other hand, are confined to a couple of avant-garde fashion designers and a few fancy restaurants in New York, so this is likely to remain a fad.

Adapted from *Brandweek.*

## Before you read

Do you think these things are trends or fads? Mark each trend (*T*) or fad (*F*).

_____ 1. casual attire

_____ 2. buying books online

_____ 3. buying groceries online

_____ 4. environmentally safe dry cleaning

_____ 5. CD players

_____ 6. surfing

_____ 7. snowboarding

_____ 8. public transportation

## Reading

Scan the text to check your answers. Then read the whole text.

## After you read

sing previous
owledge

:anning

:cognizing
idience

lessing
eaning from
intext

iderstanding
*tails

*lating
ading to
:rsonal
:perience

**A** Who do you think the text was written for? Check (✔) the correct answer.

_____ 1. economics professors

_____ 2. business people

_____ 3. bank employees

_____ 4. fashion designers

**B** Find the words and phrases in the reading that match these definitions. Write one word on each line.

1. make money from          ___cash___   ___in___   ___on___ (par. 1)

2. losing a lot of money          _____ (par. 1)

3. is more important than          _____ (par. 3)

4. availability when needed          _____ (par. 4)

5. affecting every part; spreading through _____ (par. 9)

**C** Mark each item accessible (*A*) or not accessible (*N*). Then write the reasons that the items marked *N* are not accessible.

__N__ 1. eating expensive chocolates
        _price_____

_____ 2. going skiing
        _____

_____ 3. microwave ovens
        _____

_____ 4. buying small airplanes
        _____

_____ 5. vitamin supplements
        _____

**D** Answer these questions.
1. Which things in your country do you think are fads? Which are trends?
2. Which fads were popular a few years ago but have disappeared? Why didn't they become trends?
3. What do you think some future trends will be? Why?

## Vocabulary Expansion

**A** Write the acronyms for these words.

1. central processing unit             *CPU*
2. Cable News Network
3. Music Television
4. Bachelor of Science
5. British Broadcasting Corporation
6. Master of Arts
7. National Aeronautics and Space Administration
8. Organization of Petroleum Exporting Countries
9. liquid crystal display
10. General Equivalency Diploma
11. United Nations Educational, Scientific and Cultural Organization
12. personal digital assistant

**B** Complete the diagrams with the acronyms from exercise A. Then add your own acronyms to each diagram.

*CPU*

COMPUTER
TERMS

TELEVISION
STATIONS

# ACRONYMS

ORGANIZATIONS

EDUCATIONAL
DEGREES

## Fashion and you

Work in groups. Bring in fashion magazines. Discuss which fashions are fads and which are trends. Give reasons. Then present your ideas to the class.

# U N I T 14 The media

You are going to read three texts about the media. First, answer the questions in the boxes.

**READING 1**

## Something strange is happening to tabloids

This newspaper article describes how tabloids are trying to establish credibility with the public.

1. What kinds of stories do tabloids usually cover?
2. Are tabloids popular in your country? Why or why not?
3. Is your favorite newspaper considered serious or a tabloid?

**READING 2**

## When our worlds collide

Read this magazine article to find out how journalists choose photos for news magazines.

1. What do you notice when you flip through a magazine?
2. What is the most popular subject of newspaper and magazine photos?
3. How are the pictures in newspapers different from those in tabloids?

**READING 3**

## Media violence harms children; Media violence does not harm children

This book excerpt presents opposing views on media violence.

1. Do violent movies and TV shows bother you? Why or why not?
2. Have you seen a violent movie or TV program recently?
3. Should children be allowed to watch violent programs?

### Vocabulary

Find out the meanings of the words in *italics*. Then check (✔) the statements you agree with.

_____ 1. Parents should *curb* the amount of television their children watch.
_____ 2. There's too much blood and *gore* in the movies.
_____ 3. The media has little *impact* on the way people think.
_____ 4. *Ethics* plays a large role in what the media reports.
_____ 5. News programs shouldn't *air* war *footage*.
_____ 6. Most journalists are *hypocrites*.
_____ 7. It is the media's responsibility to *mobilize* public *outrage*.
_____ 8. The media should *withhold* information that might cause panic.

# Something strange is happening to tabloids

1 It could be the most shocking tabloid story in America – and one that they can't print. Splashed across newspaper trucks making their deliveries in the northeastern states of America are the words, "No Elvis. No Aliens. No UFOs." It's not, of course, that aliens have stopped abducting, or that Elvis no longer eats at Burger King; it's just that the new management at American Media, publisher of the *National Enquirer*, the *Globe*, and the *Star*, has decided that readers will no longer be hearing of it.

2 America's tabloids are undergoing a major change under the leadership of David Pecker, a former director of a French company that publishes glossy magazines such as Elle. He believes that the way to halt the drop in readership that all the supermarket tabloids have suffered over the past decade is to take them upmarket.

3 Under Pecker, American Media is attempting to rebrand, reposition, or tweak its seven major titles to cover the spectrum from country music (*Country Weekly*) to the sensational to the super-weird: The *National Examiner* will focus on strange human interest stories; the *Star* on celebrities; the *National Enquirer* on credible, news-driven tales; the *Globe* will still feature gossip about the celebs; the *Sun* will focus on a more mature readership, with health-orientated and religious articles, and *Weekly World News* on nonsense such as the wedding of the world's fattest man.

4 Pecker has a clear idea of the role tabloids need to play to win back readership. "What tabloids stand for is to expose the hypocrisy of the rich and famous," he says. When he took over the company last year, he commissioned 5,000 consumer interviews to discover why only one out of eight people who flip through an American Media title at the supermarket buys it. The answer? "They were fascinated. But they didn't believe it."

5 On his arrival, Pecker issued an order: no more autopsy shots, no more Elvis sightings, no more UFOs. The tabloids would be entering an era of respectability, in which big-name advertisers would buy space, readers would return, and journalists would want jobs. "The easiest way to look at it is, if a big Hollywood story breaks, the *Enquirer* would do investigative stories, the Star would cover the impact on the celebrity's career, and the *Globe* would really do the spicy parts of the story," Pecker says.

6 After the decision to ban ads for psychic healers and miracle remedies, the titles have begun to attract new advertisers. The *Enquirer* has been redesigned with a sleeker, all-color look. In line with a new *Enquirer* slogan, "Get it first. Get it fast. Get it right," old-style headlines such as "Kills Pal and Eats Pieces of Flesh" have been toned down.

7 Many doubt that United States tabloids can really change. "I can't imagine a transformation that would give them credibility," says Bob Steele, a specialist in journalistic ethics. "Good for them if they want to respect themselves. The question remains: What do they stand for as a news organization?"

8 Five million Americans who buy Pecker's tabloids know exactly why they do so, even if they don't believe everything they read. Will tamer tabloids succeed? Pecker thinks so. But there will be no Elvis.

Adapted from *The Guardian*.

## Before you read

Check (✔) the subjects that appear in tabloids.

_____ 1. sightings of Elvis Presley      _____ 5. health-related articles

_____ 2. sightings of aliens      _____ 6. bizarre wedding stories

_____ 3. sightings of UFOs      _____ 7. ads for psychic healers

_____ 4. celebrity gossip      _____ 8. ads for miracle cures

## Reading

Scan the text to find out which subjects above will no longer be in American tabloids. Then read the whole text.

## After you read

**A** Find the words and phrases in the reading that match these definitions. Write one word on each line.

1. put an end to      ___*halt*___ (par. 2)

2. change slightly      _____ (par. 3)

3. represent      _____ (par. 4)

4. not allow      _____ (par. 6)

5. made less forceful or offensive      _____ (par. 6)

6. less exciting      _____ (par. 8)

**B** Where do you think the headlines could appear? Match each headline with a tabloid. (Note: In some cases more than one answer is possible.)

a. *National Enquirer*    c. *Sun*    e. *Weekly World News*    g. *Globe*
b. *National Examiner*    d. *Star*    f. *Country Weekly*

__ 1. **Quintuplets' Mom and Dad Say Five Babies Are Not Enough**

__ 2. **VITAMIN E is the Secret to Looking Years Younger**

__ 3. *President's Son Arrested for Assault*

__ 4. **DOLLY Wins Major Country Music Awards Again**

__ 5. **WORLD'S TALLEST WOMAN WEDS WORLD'S SHORTEST MAN**

__ 6. **Find Out How These Hollywood Stars Got Their Start**

__ 7. **Why Husband Number Six No Longer Wants Liz**

**C** Answer these questions.

1. What is the most outrageous story you ever saw or read about in a tabloid?
2. Which of the newspapers mentioned in the text would you most likely read? Why?
3. Should any kinds of stories be banned from newspapers and magazines? If so, which?

# When our **worlds** collide

1 "Wanna buy a body?" That was the opening line of more than a few phone calls I got from freelance photographers when I was a photo editor at *U.S. News.* Like many in the mainstream press, I wanted to separate the world of photographers into "them," who trade in pictures of bodies or chase celebrities like Princess Diana, and "us," the serious newspeople. But after 16 years in that role, I came to wonder whether the two worlds were easily distinguishable.

2 Working in the reputable world of journalism, I assigned photographers to cover other people's nightmares. I justified invading moments of grief, under the guise of the reader's right to know. I didn't ask photographers to trespass or to stalk, but I didn't have to: I worked with pros who did what others did, talking their way into situations or shooting from behind police lines, to get pictures I was after. And I wasn't alone.

3 In any American town, in the aftermath of a car crash or some other hideous incident when ordinary people are hurt or killed, you rarely see photographers pushing, paparazzi-like, past rescue workers to capture the blood and gore. But you are likely to see local newspaper and television photographers on the scene – and fast. . . .

4 How can we justify doing this? Journalists are taught to separate doing the job from worrying about the consequences of publishing what they record. Repeatedly, they are reminded of a news-business dictum: Leave your conscience in the office. You get the picture or the footage; the decision whether to print or air it comes later. A victim may lie bleeding, unconscious, or dead: Your job is to record the image. You're a photographer, not a paramedic. You put away your emotions and document the scene.

5 Bringing out the worst. We act this way partly because we know that the pictures can have important meaning. Photographs can change deplorable situations by mobilizing public outrage or increasing public understanding. . . .

6 But catastrophic events often bring out the worst in photographers and photo editors. In the first minutes and hours after a disaster occurs, photo agencies . . . buy pictures. They rush to obtain exclusive rights to dramatic images and death is usually the subject . . . . Often, an agency buys a picture from a local newspaper or an amateur photographer and puts it up for bid by major magazines. The most keenly sought "exclusives" command tens of thousands of dollars through bidding contests.

7 I worked on all those stories and many like them. When they happen, you move quickly: buying, dealing, assigning, trying to beat the agencies to the pictures. I rarely felt the impact of the story, at least until the coverage was over. . . .

8 Now, many people believe journalists are the hypocrites who need to be brought down, and it's our pictures that most gall. Readers may not believe, as we do, that there is a distinction between sober-minded "us" and sleazy "them." In too many cases, by our choices of images as well as how we get them, we prove our readers right.

From *US News & World Report.*

> **READING TIP**
> Sometimes ellipsis (…) is used to show that words, phrases, or sentences have been omitted from a reading. For example, the ellipsis after the words *and fast* (par. 3) indicate that sentences were omitted from the original paragraph.

redicting

kimming

estating

Making
nferences

Relating
eading to
ersonal
xperience

## Before you read

Read the first paragraph on the opposite page. Then check (✔) the statement that you think best describes the writer's opinion.

_____ 1. Mainstream journalists are more ethical than tabloid photographers.

_____ 2. Mainstream journalists are no more ethical than tabloid photographers.

_____ 3. Mainstream journalists are less ethical than tabloid photographers.

## Reading

Skim the text to check your prediction. Then read the whole text.

## After you read

**A** Underline the sentences in the text that have the same meaning as the sentences below.

1. I told myself that shooting people at sad times was my way of informing the public. (par. 2)
   _I justified invading moments of grief under the guise of the reader's right to know._
2. Journalists covering a news story aren't supposed to think about whether they're doing the right thing. (par. 4)
3. Sometimes journalists can help people by showing the photographs. (par. 5)
4. Editors pay a lot of money for photos that their competitors want. (par. 6)
5. Only after the story was out of the news did I think about the pictures. (par. 7)
6. The public doesn't trust or respect people in the news business. (par. 8)

**B** Check (✔) the statements that are true.

   ✓ 1. Other photo editors have done the same thing the writer did.

   _____ 2. People who appeared in the writer's photos wrote him angry letters.

   _____ 3. Pictures taken at scenes where someone dies do not end up in print.

   _____ 4. People in news photos are not always asked whether their pictures can be taken.

   _____ 5. The writer wants to apologize to some people in the pictures he used.

   _____ 6. The writer now works for the tabloid press.

   _____ 7. The writer still feels guilty about some of the things he has done for his job.

**C** Answer these questions.

1. Do you think photographs play an important role in telling a news story? Do you remember a photo that had a strong impact on you?
2. Do newspapers in your country print photographs of catastrophic events? Do you think they should? Why or why not?
3. Do you think journalism is a respectable profession? Why or why not?

# Media violence harms children

1    The debate is over. Violence on television and in the movies is damaging to children. Forty years of research conclude that repeated exposure to high levels of media violence teaches some children and adolescents to settle interpersonal differences with violence, while teaching many more to be indifferent to this solution. Under the media's influence, children at younger and younger ages are using violence as a first, not a last, resort to conflict.

2    Locked away in professional journals are thousands of articles documenting the negative effects of media, particularly media violence, on our nation's youth. Children who are heavy viewers of television are more aggressive, more pessimistic, weigh more, are less imaginative, and less capable students than their lighter-viewing counterparts. With an increasing sense of urgency, parents are confronting the fact that the "real story" about media violence and its effects on children has been withheld.

3    Leonard Eron, one of the country's most important experts on media and children, has said that:

> There can no longer be any doubt that heavy exposure to televised violence is one of the causes of aggressive behavior, crime, and violence in society. The evidence comes from both the laboratory and real-life studies. Television violence affects youngsters of all ages, of both genders, at all socioeconomic levels, and all levels of intelligence. The effect is not limited to children who are already disposed to being aggressive and is not restricted to this country.

4    Every major group concerned with children has studied and issued reports on the effects of media violence on children. Many have called for curbing television and movie violence. Doctors, therapists, teachers, and youth workers all find themselves struggling to help youngsters who, influenced by repeated images of quick, celebratory violence, find it increasingly difficult to deal with the inevitable frustrations of daily life.

# Media violence does not harm children

5    One of the reasons we have so much trouble understanding complicated issues like supposed connections between culture and violence . . . is that so many "experts" are thrown at us, often offering contradictory conclusions.

6    But some experts have better credentials than others. Harvard psychiatrist Robert Coles, no fan of TV violence, has been studying and writing about the moral, spiritual, and developmental lives of children for much of his life. His works have been widely praised and circulated as new, insightful looks at kids' complex inner lives. Parents worried about the impact culture has on their kids should ignore the headlines and read *The Moral Life of Children*. They would know more and feel better.

7    A young moviegoer, Coles writes, can repeatedly be exposed to the "excesses of a Hollywood genre" – sentimentality, violence, the misrepresentation of history, racial stereotypes, pure simplemindedness – and emerge unharmed intellectually as well as morally. In fact, sometimes these images help the child to "sort matters out, stop and think about what is true and what is not by any means true – in the past, in the present." The child, says Coles, "doesn't forget what he's learned in school, learned at home, from hearing people talk in his family and his neighborhood."

8    Culture offers important moments for moral reflection, and it ought not to be used as an occasion for "overwrought psychiatric comment," Coles warns, or for making simpleminded connections between films and "the collective American conscience."

Adapted from *Media Violence: Opposing Viewpoints*.

## Before you read

edicting

**Look at the two headlines on the opposite page and the ideas below. Which text do
you think each idea is from? Mark each statement first text (*A*) or second text (*B*).**

_____ 1. "Excesses of a Hollywood genre" won't hurt young moviegoers.

_____ 2. Watching a lot of television causes aggression, pessimism, and obesity.

_____ 3. Television violence affects all children, regardless of age, gender, or intelligence.

_____ 4. Children remember what they learn from teachers, parents, and others.

## Reading

:anning

**Scan the text to check your predictions. Then read the whole text.**

## After you read

uessing
eaning from
ontext

**A** **Find the words in *italics* in the reading. Then match each word with its meaning.**

_____ 1. *settle differences* (par. 1)      a. showing clear understanding

_____ 2. *indifferent to* (par. 1)      b. likely to

__d__ 3. *last resort* (par. 1)      c. unconcerned about

_____ 4. *disposed to* (par. 3)      d. end arguments

_____ 5. *credentials* (par. 6)      e. ability and experience

_____ 6. *insightful* (par. 6)      f. final source of help

nderstanding
omplex
entences

**B** **Separate each sentence from the text into two or three new sentences.**

1. (par. 4) Doctors, *therapists, teachers, and youth workers all find themselves struggling to help*
   youngsters. These youngsters are *influenced by repeated images of quick, celebratory violence.*
   As a result, they *find it increasingly difficult to deal with the inevitable frustrations* of daily life.

2. (par. 5) We have a lot of trouble _____.
   One of the reasons is that _____.
   These experts often _____.

3. (par. 6) Some parents are worried _____.
   These parents should _____.

nderstanding
ain ideas

**C** **Write (*A*) for the statement that best expresses the main idea of the first text.
Write (*B*) for the statement that best expresses the main idea of the second text.**

_____ 1. A lot more research on the subject of media violence is still needed.

_____ 2. People often change their minds after they study media violence more carefully.

_____ 3. Experts overwhelmingly agree that media violence has harmful effects.

elating
ading to
ersonal
xperience

**D** **Answer these questions.**

1. Do you think media violence is harmful to children and adolescents? Why or why not?
2. Should children stop watching violent movies? Why or why not?
3. In general, do you think the media has a positive or negative effect on children? Why?

## Vocabulary expansion

**A** Read the definitions. Then complete the words using the prefixes *counter-*, *mis-*, or *inter-*.

1. *counter* **part:** a person or thing with the same function as another person or thing
2. _____ **personal:** occurring among or involving different people
3. _____ **represent:** describe something written or said incorrectly
4. _____ **continental:** between continents
5. _____ **productive:** producing the opposite effect of what you want
6. _____ **attack:** attack someone who has attacked you
7. _____ **behave:** behave badly
8. _____ **inform:** give someone incorrect information
9. _____ **national:** between countries
10. _____ **understand:** not understand something correctly
11. _____ **related:** connected to each other
12. _____ **clockwise:** in the opposite direction to the hands on a clock

**B** Complete the sentences with words from exercise A. Be sure to use the correct word form.

1. The problems are ___*interrelated*___ . They can't be separated.

2. We ran around the track in a _____ direction.

3. I _____ his directions, so I got lost.

4. He can't control his children when they _____ .

5. The meeting was _____ . People were arguing instead of coming up with a plan.

6. She has good _____ skills. She can work well with all kinds of people.

7. The Mexican Foreign Minister met his Canadian and American _____ .

8. The United Nations is an _____ organization.

9. The politician is angry because he thinks reporters _____ what he says.

10. I was told the meeting is today, not tomorrow. I must have been _____ .

11. I always get tired on _____ flights. The time difference bothers me.

12. When the soldiers attacked the fortress, the people _____ by using arrows.

## The media and you

Work in small groups. Do a survey of people's opinion of the media. First, come up with five questions.

Example: *Do you think there is too much violence on TV?*

*Do you ever read tabloids?*

Then ask five classmates, friends, or family members. Report your findings to the class.

# 15 Art

You are going to read three texts about art. First, answer the questions in the boxes.

**READING 1**

## Girl with a Pitcher

This excerpt from a novel reveals how one artist sees and describes the colors he uses to paint.

1. Think of a famous painting. Can you visualize its colors?
2. What colors do you see when you look out the window?
3. What process do you think an artist follows to paint a portrait?

**READING 2**

## Organic architecture

Read this newspaper article to learn about a movement that draws inspiration from the beauty and harmony of nature.

1. Have you ever seen unusual architecture? Why is it interesting?
2. Where do you think architects get their inspiration for new designs?
3. What features characterize "good architecture?"

**READING 3**

## How forgeries corrupt our top museums

The writer of this magazine article considers the question, "Are the works of art in museums genuine or fake?"

1. Do you like to visit museums? Why or why not?
2. Which museum in your city or town has a famous art collection?
3. Can you tell the difference between real and fake art? If so, how?

## Vocabulary

Find out the meanings of the words in *italics*. Then check (✔) the magazine where you would find each article.

|  | Museums Today | Modern Architecture |
|---|---|---|
| 1. New Ways to Display *Artifacts* |  |  |
| 2. *Curators* in the News |  |  |
| 3. Buildings' *Curves* and *Straight Lines* |  |  |
| 4. Secret *Hoards* of Ancient Art |  |  |
| 5. *Structures* and *Landscapes* |  |  |
| 6. Recent *Sculpture* Exhibitions |  |  |

# Girl with a Pitcher

1    I reluctantly set out the colors he asked for each morning. One day I put out a blue as well. The second time I laid it out he said to me, "No ultramarine, Griet. Only the colors I asked for. Why did you set it out when I did not ask for it?" He was annoyed.

2    "I'm sorry, sir. It's just –" I took a deep breath – "she is wearing a blue skirt. I thought you would want it, rather than leaving it black."

3    "When I am ready, I will ask."

4    I nodded and turned back to polishing the lion-head chair. My chest hurt. I did not want him to be angry at me.

5    He opened the middle window, filling the room with cold air.

6    "Come here, Griet."

7    I set my rag on the sill and went to him.

8    "Look out the window."

9    I looked out. It was a breezy day, with clouds disappearing behind the New Church tower.

10    "What color are those clouds?"

11    "Why, white, sir."

12    He raised his eyebrows slightly. "Are they?"

13    I glanced at them. "And grey. Perhaps it will snow."

14    "Come, Griet, you can do better than that. Think of your vegetables."

15    "My vegetables, sir?"

16    He moved his head slightly. I was annoying him again. My jaw tightened.

17    "Think of how you separated the whites. Your turnips and your onions – are they the same white?"

18    Suddenly I understood. "No. The turnip has green in it, the onion yellow."

19    "Exactly. Now, what colors do you see in the clouds?"

20    "There is some blue in them," I said after studying them for a few minutes. "And – yellow as well. And there is some green!" I became so excited I actually pointed. I had been looking at clouds all my life, but I felt as if I saw them for the first time at that moment.

21    He smiled. "You will find there is little pure white in clouds, yet people say they are white. Now do you understand why I do not need the blue yet?"

22    "Yes, sir." I did not really understand, but did not want to admit it. I felt I almost knew.

23    When at last he began to add colors on top of the false colors, I saw what he meant. He painted a light blue over the girl's skirt, and it became a blue through which bits of black could be seen, darker in the shadow of the table, lighter closer to the window. To the wall areas he added yellow ocher, through which some of the grey showed. It became a bright but not a white wall. When the light shone on the wall, I discovered, it was not white, but many colors.

24    The pitcher and basin were the most complicated—they became yellow, and brown, and green, and blue. They reflected the pattern of the rug, the girl's bodice, the blue cloth draped over the chair—everything but their true silver color. And yet they looked as they should, like a pitcher and a basin.

25    After that I could not stop looking at things.

Johannes Vermeer (Dutch, 1632–1675), *Young Woman with a Water Pitcher,* 1664–1665.

From *Girl with a Pearl Earring.*

## Before you read

**Look at the picture on the opposite page. Then match the parts of the painting with the colors you think the artist used to paint them.**

a. black      c. brown      e. grey      g. red      i. white
b. blue       d. green      f. yellow    h. silver   j. ocher (yellow-orange)

1. the girl's blue skirt _____

2. the silver pitcher and basin _____

3. the white wall _____

## Reading

**Scan the text to check your predictions. Then read the whole text.**

## After you read

**A** | **Where does the text probably come from? Check (✔) the correct answer.**

_____ 1. a novel about an artist          _____ 3. a manual for beginning painters

_____ 2. a textbook about European art    _____ 4. a book about modern art

**B** | **Compare the meaning of each pair of sentences. Write same (S) or different (D).**

_D_ 1. I reluctantly set out the colors he asked for each morning.
     Every morning, I was happy to lay out his paints.

_____ 2. I had been looking at clouds all my life, but I felt as if I saw them for the
        first time.
        For the first time in my life, I really noticed clouds.

_____ 3. I did not really understand [the artist], but did not want to admit it.
        I didn't want the artist to know I did not understand what he meant.

_____ 4. When the light shone on the wall, it was not white, but many colors.
        The light shining on the wall made it appear to have many colors.

_____ 5. They looked as they should, like a picture and a basin.
        The pitcher and basin should have looked better.

**C** | **Answer the questions.**

1. Who is Griet?
2. What kind of person is Griet?
3. What kind of person is the artist?
4. Why did the artist tell Griet she could "do better than that" ? (par. 14)
5. Why does Griet say she "could not stop looking at things" after that? (par. 23)

**D** | **Answer these questions.**

1. Who is your favorite artist? What do you like about the artist's work?
2. If you were going to paint the place where you are now, what colors would you use?
3. Is it important for children to learn about art? If so, where should it be taught? If
   not, why not?

# Organic architecture

1 When architect Douglas Cardinal was studying at the University of Texas 40 years ago, he used to drive to the school through the Rockies from his home in Alberta, Canada. "I took a new route every time and was inspired by those forms," the 67-year-old Cardinal recently told an American journalist. "They helped me realize architecture should stem from the natural environment of a place."

2 While Canadians are familiar with Cardinal's highly original work, he is not alone in taking inspiration from nature and preferring curves to straight lines. As a key contributor to an international movement known as organic architecture, his work and views are prominently featured in *The New Organic Architecture: The Breaking Wave*. There is no simple definition of organic architecture. But British architect and author David Pearson attempts to convey the meaning of the term with examples of fascinating buildings by 30 contemporary architects from 15 countries.

3 These imaginative structures share common characteristics: they draw inspiration from natural forms and strive to apply ecological science to how the buildings are lit, heated, and cooled. They harmonize with the landscape and express the human spirit.

4 For example, on the South Pacific island of New Caledonia, Italian architect Renzo Piano has designed a stunning jungle village inspired by native huts and their relationship to nature. These mysterious, soaring wood structures resemble wicker baskets or giant curved barrels, and are designed for natural ventilation.

5 In Palm Springs, California, American architect Kendrick Bangs Kellogg has created a desert house whose roof canopies emulate a giant fungus. From another angle, its curved concrete wings make the house look like a prehistoric bird rising from the landscape. The house is earthquake-proof and captures and stores the sun's heat, releasing it at night.

6 "There's a growing awareness of the need for all architects to impact as little as possible on the environment," Pearson, 60, said in an interview from his London office. "What is new is to link the newer environmental awareness to the passionate design that can come out of looking at nature and its forms."

7 Pearson is reminded of the natural world in a wide range of remarkable buildings that demonstrate the diversity of the organic approach; he sees it in the wing-like detail of the spire of a Roman Catholic church in Hungary by Imre Makovecz; the extraordinary bubble-shaped domes of the new Eden Project

botanical center in Cornwall, England, by Nicholas Grimshaw; and, again, in an ocean-view California house by Bart Prince that sprawls like an exquisite piece of driftwood.

8 "Organic architecture is rooted in a passion for life, nature, and natural forms," Pearson writes. "Emphasizing beauty and harmony, its free-flowing curves and expressive forms are sympathetic to the human body, mind, and spirit. In a well-designed 'organic' building, we feel better and freer."

9 Cardinal recently won an award for a turtle-shaped civic center and is also designing an interpretative center for the site of a 9,000-year-old village in British Columbia. The shape of the interpretive center suggests the curving body of a salmon, the swirls of a mollusk, and wavy patterns of sand created by tides.

10 "There's an infinite variety of forms in nature and I am continually inspired by observing all these forms," says Cardinal.

Adapted from *The Ottawa Citizen.*

inking about
rsonal
xperience

anning

nderstanding
ference
ords

nderstanding
etails

elating
ading to
rsonal
xperience

## Before you read

Look at the title on the opposite page and the words and phrases below.
Then write what *organic architecture* means to you.

the Rockies                turtle-shaped
a giant fungus             the curving body of a salmon
a prehistoric bird         the swirls of a mollusk
driftwood                  wavy patterns of sand created by tides

organic architecture: _____

## Reading

Scan the text to check your definition. Then read the whole text.

## After you read

**A** What do these words refer to?

1. *those forms* (par. 1, line 8)                          *the Rockies*
2. *They* (par. 1, line 10)                                 _____
3. *These imaginative structures* (par. 3, line 1)         _____
4. *its* (par. 5, line 6)                                   _____
5. *it* (par. 5, line 12)                                   _____
6. *its* (par. 6, line 10)                                  _____
7. *its* (par. 8, line 5)                                   _____

**B** Complete the chart. Write (?) if the text doesn't give the information.

|                | Picture 1 | Picture 2 | Picture 3 | Picture 4 |
|----------------|-----------|-----------|-----------|-----------|
| a. Architect   | *Renzo Piano* |       |           |           |
| b. Location    |           |           |           |           |
| c. Resembles   |           |           |           |           |

**C** Answer these questions.

1. What do you think of the structures in the pictures?
2. Are there any examples of organic architecture in your country? If so, where? If not, which of the of these buildings would best fit into the landscape?
3. What instructions would you give an architect to design your ideal home?

# How forgeries corrupt our *museums*

1 For several years, the art trade in London has been flooded with rumors about a fabulous secret hoard of ancient Middle Eastern silver. Called the "treasure of the western cave" and dating from the sixth century B.C., it is said to be on the market at the premises of a dealer. It was allegedly discovered "by peasants" in a cave in the western highlands of Iran. Out of between 200 and 600 pieces, only a few have so far "surfaced," and one or two have ended up in the Miho Museum in Japan.

2 The Iranians were very angry that they managed to seize only part of the hoard and that the rest was smuggled abroad. But now they may worry less. The academic journal Source has just produced evidence that at least one piece in the Miho is a fake.

3 Fakes have always been known to exist in the world of antiquities, but what is now emerging is the astonishing scale of them. A report from the Archaeological Institute of America concludes that no less than 80 percent of all "ancient" West African sculpture on the market are fake. This report identifies individual forgers and names dealers in western European capitals whom these forgers supply.

4 How can this "forgery culture" flourish? The answer is to be found in the fact that about 80 percent of the artifacts that pass through the antiquities trade have no definite provenance. In other words, it is not known where they were found and therefore, even if they are genuine, they can tell us little about ancient history.

5 People in the trade say that most of these objects were found in "casual discoveries." Shamefully, they know that this is not true. They advance the fiction because it suits their commercial purposes. The reality is that the artifacts come from looting, not by local farmers "happening" on a few finds, but by organized gangs of criminals using such tools as mechanical diggers to destroy whole sites in their indiscriminate search for saleable items.

6 The "treasure of the western cave" is a classic example of how faking works. Undoubtedly, there is somewhere a hoard of genuine silver, though what date it is, and where exactly it comes from, are unknown. But there are also plenty of complete fakes on the market, together with partial imitations – genuine but plain artifacts, embellished with modern, fake decoration. Either way, the archaeological record is corrupted.

7 Faking is big business, and is of such a standard that even the greatest scholars may be fooled some of the time. The antiquities trade likes to play down not only the extent of looting and faking, but also the overlap between the two. These latest reports let the cat out of the bag. But it is the overlap with plundered antiquities that is the most significant factor, and which leads to the culture of forgery.

8 These twin evils have already corrupted the archaeological record more than we can ever know. Collectors of antiquities – whether private individuals or curators in museums – need to be aware that they not only aid the plunder of potentially invaluable sites, but put themselves at the mercy of fakers as well. They are being not just dishonest, but foolish.

Adapted from *New Statesman.*

**READING TIP** Writers sometimes use quotation marks to show irony, or the opposite meaning of the words. For example, the writer puts quotation marks around *by peasants* (par. 1) to mean he doesn't think the silver was discovered by peasants.

edicting

anning

cognizing
ne

essing
eaning from
ntext

derstanding
mplex
ntences

lating
ading to
rsonal
perience

## Before you read

**Look at the title on the opposite page and the following sentences from the text. Then check (✔) the statement below that you think best describes the writer's opinion.**

*An astonishing number of fakes is now emerging in the world of antiquities. Faking is big business, and is of such a standard that even scholars may be fooled. Faking and looting have corrupted the archaeological record more than we know.*

_____ 1. People who smuggle art out of a country should be put in jail.

_____ 2. Museums that display forgeries should be shut down.

_____ 3. What is happening in the art world is shameful.

## Reading

**Scan the text to check your prediction. Then read the whole text**

## After you read

**A** **The following phrases express irony. Write the writer's intended meaning beside each quote.**

1. "by peasants" (par. 1)     *Peasants didn't really find the silver.*

2. "surfaced" (par. 1)     _____

3. "ancient" (par. 3)     _____

4. "casual discoveries" (par. 5)     _____

**B** **Find the words and phrases in the reading that match these definitions. Write one word on each line.**

1. stated as a fact but without proof     _____ (par. 1)

2. place of origin     *allegedly*  (par. 4)

3. promote a lie     _____ _____ _____ (par. 5)

4. decorated     _____ (par. 6)

**C** **Find the answers to the questions. Then underline them in the text.**

1. What is the "treasure of the western cave"? (par. 1, 9 words)
   *a fabulous secret hoard of ancient Middle Eastern silver*
2. What has no definite provenance? (par. 4, 12 words)
3. Who "finds" the artifacts? (par. 5, 4 words)
4. Who collects antiquities? (par. 8, 6 words)

**D** **Answer these questions.**

1. Do you think people who make and sell copies of famous art are criminals? Why or why not?
2. Would you like your favorite work of art less if you found out it was fake? Why or why not?
3. Should people who steal antiquities be punished? If so, how?

## Vocabulary expansion

**A** Compound adjectives consist of two or more words that are often hyphenated.

Examples: *184-page* book (a book *that has 184 pages*)
*turtle-shaped* civic center (a civic center *that is shaped like a turtle*)
*9,000-year-old* village (a village *that is 9,000 years old*)

**Change the phrases in *italics* into compound adjectives.**

1. An object *that is in the shape of an egg* is an ___egg-shaped___ object.

2. A window *that is in the shape of a star* is a _____ window.

3. An artist *who paints with his left hand* is _____ .

4. A boy *who has blue eyes* is _____ .

5. A woman *who has long hair* is _____ .

6. A painting *that is 200 years old* is a _____ painting.

7. An artist *who is 25 years old* is a _____ artist.

8. A museum catalogue *that has 175 pages* is a _____ book.

**B** Make compound adjectives with the words in parentheses. Then write a sentence with each compound adjective.

1. shape    *box-shaped*    *My house is box-shaped.*

2. hair    _____    _____

3. eye    _____    _____

4. hand    _____    _____

5. old    _____    _____

6. page    _____    _____

## Art and you

Work in groups. Imagine you are going to show visitors your country's greatest works of art. The works of art can be paintings, statues, or buildings. They can be in museums or public places such as parks. First, decide what the visitors should see. Then prepare short descriptions of the works of art.

## UNIT

# 16 Humor

You are going to read three texts about humor. First, answer the questions in the boxes.

## So, who's the comedian?

Read this newspaper article written by someone who tried stand-up comedy.

1. Do you like stand-up comedy? Why or why not?
2. Do you think you are funny?
3. Is it possible to learn to be funny? If so, how?

## Taking humor seriously in the workplace

Does humor have a role in the workplace? This website looks for some connections.

1. Can humor in the workplace improve relationships between colleagues? If so, how?
2. Is it important for people to laugh at work? Why or why not?
3. Why do you think people sometimes make fun of themselves?

## Three comedians

Read how three well-known American comedians translate their humor into print.

1. Which stand-up comics are popular in your country?
2. Who are your favorite comedians? Why do they make you laugh?
3. What do you think is the funniest TV show?

### Vocabulary

**Find out the meanings of the words and phrases in *italics*. Then answer the questions.**

1. Do you think you could *bring down the house* by telling jokes?
2. Have you ever spoken into a *mike (microphone)*?
3. Have you ever performed *onstage*?
4. Do you ever *poke fun at* yourself?
5. Does your favorite comedian usually use *props*?
6. Have you ever seen an audience *rolling in the aisles*?
7. Do you think all good comedians have *spontaneity*?
8. Do you think all good comedians have *stage presence*?

# So, who's the comedian?

1 According to a recent poll, 84 percent of American men believe they are funnier than the average stand-up comic, and that if they ever got up behind a mike they'd bring down the house.

2 I just made up that poll, but literal truth is inessential to being a stand-up comic, which I now am. I became a stand-up comic at 12:45 yesterday afternoon when I walked onto a comedy club stage and did a "bit." It was an audition in which professional and semi-pro comedians had exactly two minutes each to perform for a big-shot producer.

3 During my two minutes, I learned many things about the craft of comedy, the main ones being:

- Two minutes is a very, very, excruciatingly long time.

- You should always remember not to inhale beads covered with spit, because you can die.

4 But I am getting ahead of myself.

5 I am not a comic, have never appeared onstage, am awkward before a mike, have no spontaneity, and basically no interpersonal skills. But I have written some funny things in the newspapers, and I figured that if you can write funny, you can be funny. That was my first mistake.

6 My second mistake was not staying in my seat when my name was called. Good stand-up comics hone their acts over months if not years, polishing them before bathroom mirrors, their friends, etc. I developed the key element of mine the morning I went on. The last thing I did before I left the house was bring a box full of plastic beads, because I figured they could be a prop for something.

7 For the first few seconds of my two minutes, I was simply staring forward, mouth agape, expressing the concept: "Uuungh."

8 Finally:

9 "This is the debut of my career as a professional stand-up comic. It's a kind of a special moment for me. I'd like to take this opportunity to say something to my mother, who was an inspiration to me throughout my life. My mother passed away a few years ago, but I feel she is still with me. All the time, wherever I go, I feel her presence. Day in and day out. So I would like to say this to her. LEAVE ME ALONE, MA!"

10 Some people actually laughed.

11 Then I said, "Anyway, this really is my first time onstage, and I'm pretty insecure because, y'know, I'm not all that funny and I have a really lousy stage presence . . ."

12 People were laughing. Yes, I realize they were mostly laughing about how bad I was.

13 "But I've been working on the problem. A long time ago a Greek guy named Demosthenes had the same problem I have, and he became a great orator by sticking pebbles in his mouth, so I thought I would (and here I began putting the beads in my mouth) try that. See, the idea is that if you can talk through the pebbles (now I was stuffing them in by the handful) you can learn to . . ."

14 More laughter.

15 ". . . talk better and wfnm fmuff frmphm grphnm fprm . . ."

16 I looked at my watch, said something that might have sounded like "My time is up," and left to somewhat spirited applause. What the audience did not know was that I was quietly choking on a slippery bead.

Adapted from *The Washington Post*.

## Before you read

inking about
rsonal
perience

Look at the picture on the opposite page. What do you think the comic is doing?
Do you think this is funny?

## Reading

imming

Skim the text to find out what the writer did during his comedy act. Then read the
whole text.

## After you read

cognizing
ne

**A** What is the tone of the text? Check (✔) the correct answer.

_____ 1. frightened          _____ 3. serious

_____ 2. funny               _____ 4. upset

ıessing
eaning from
ntext

**B** Find the words in *italics* in the reading. Then match each word with its meaning.
(Be careful! There is one extra answer.)

_e_ 1. *big-shot* (par. 2)          a. lively

_____ 2. *excruciatingly* (par. 3)   b. make perfect

_____ 3. *awkward* (par. 5)        c. oversize

_____ 4. *hone* (par. 6)           d. painfully

_____ 5. *agape* (par. 7)          e. important

_____ 6. *spirited* (par. 16)      f. uncomfortable

                                     g. open wide

ıderstanding
etails

**C** Check (✔) the remarks that people in the audience might have made.

_____ 1. Isn't he the guy who writes a funny newspaper column?

_____ 2. We saw that guy onstage here a couple of months ago.

_____ 3. He seemed really nervous, didn't he?

_____ 4. Wasn't that a stupid song he sang?

_____ 5. Why did he talk with those things in his mouth?

_____ 6. Everyone was rolling in the aisles!

elating
ading to
ersonal
xperience

**D** Answer these questions.

1. If you were a friend of the writer, what would you have told him about his
   performance?
2. Do men and women make equally good comedians? Do they tell jokes about the
   same things? What examples can you give?
3. If you were going to perform stand-up comedy, what would your act be about?

# Taking humor seriously in the workplace

1 How serious can we be about humor in the workplace, and how humorous can we be about the seriousness we often find there? According to a survey, only 15 percent of workers are fired because of lack of competence. The remaining 85 percent are let go because of their inability to get along with fellow employees. When asked about the qualities of an effective employee, human relations personnel say humor is a choice attribute.

2 Why has humor become a recognized asset in the workplace? Humor facilitates communication, builds relationships, reduces stress, provides perspective, and promotes attendance and energy.

## Humor facilitates communication

3 Humor provides a non-threatening way for an employee or employer to communicate without causing emotional strain on the relationship. Consider the frazzled secretary who posts the sign "I have only two speeds. If this one isn't fast enough, you're not going to like my other one." Or the somewhat scattered boss whose messy desk has the sign, "A Creative Mess is Better than Tidy Idleness." The message is clear, yet the communication is done in a light and, therefore, less stressful way. The secretary's sign pokes fun at the situation, and the boss's note pokes fun at himself.

## Humor builds relationships

4 Humor can facilitate staff cohesion and a sense of team effort in the workplace. Bulletin boards, electronic mail, intra-office memos, and voicemail are all mediums through which we can share humor with co-workers. Office jokes that take the seriousness of work lightly give us the opportunity to become more connected with others.

## Humor reduces stress

5 Work is often associated with stress, and stress is one of the main causes of illness, absenteeism, and employee burnout. Humor helps relieve stress because it makes us feel good, and we can't feel good and feel stressed simultaneously. At the moment we experience humor, feelings like depression, anger, and anxiety dissolve. When we laugh we feel physically better, and after laughter we feel happier and more relaxed. In addition, humor helps reduce psychological stress.

## Humor provides perspective

6 Humor also oils the wheels of the workplace by providing perspective. Ashleigh Brilliant (known for his one-liners on postcards) says, "Distance doesn't really make you any smaller, but it does make you part of a bigger picture." Consider the Ziggy cartoon where Ziggy is lying on the psychiatrist's couch and the psychiatrist is saying, "The whole world isn't against you . . . there are BILLIONS of people who don't care one way or the other."

## Humor promotes attention and energy

7 Humor wakes us up and increases our attention. An office bulletin board full of cartoons, one-liners, jokes, and funny pictures is one way to invite humor into the workplace. A few moments of humor at work can lead to increased productivity as the newly energized employee returns to his or her task.

8 In working environments where humor is supported, a culture develops that uses humor to reduce stress and provide perspective. Learning to laugh at ourselves and our work lightens the load.

**READING TIP** Sometimes you can guess the meaning of a word in a series by looking at words around it. For example, from the phrase *cartoons, one-liners, jokes, and funny pictures* (par. 7), you can guess that a *one-liner* is something funny.

Adapted from *www.humormatters.com/articles/workplace/htm.*

## Before you read

Relating to the topic

**Mark each statement true (*T*) or false (*F*).**

\_\_\_\_\_ 1. It's a bad idea to use humor with your coworkers.

\_\_\_\_\_ 2. People who work together feel closer if they share jokes.

\_\_\_\_\_ 3. Laughter causes physical and psychological problems.

\_\_\_\_\_ 4. Humor helps people see their problems as less important.

## Reading

Scanning

**Scan the text to check your answers. Then read the whole text.**

## After you read

Understanding main ideas

**A** **Check (✔) the statement that you think best expresses the main idea of the text.**

\_\_\_\_\_ 1. People who take humor seriously are more effective employees.

\_\_\_\_\_ 2. Humor makes work less stressful, more cohesive, and more productive.

\_\_\_\_\_ 3. People who have a sense of humor get along better with their coworkers.

Recognizing similarity in meaning

**B** **Match each word or phrase with a word or phrase that is similar in meaning.**

\_\_*c*\_\_ 1. *fired* (par. 1)          a. *staff* (par. 4)

\_\_\_\_\_ 2. *personnel* (par. 1)      b. *asset* (par. 2)

\_\_\_\_\_ 3. *attribute* (par. 1)      c. *let go* (par. 1)

\_\_\_\_\_ 4. *facilitates* (par. 2)     d. *stressed* (par. 5)

\_\_\_\_\_ 5. *frazzled* (par. 3)       e. *promotes* (par. 2)

\_\_\_\_\_ 6. *relieve* (par. 5)        f. *reduce* (par. 5)

Restating

**C** **Compare the meaning of each pair of sentences. Write same (*S*) or different (*D*).**

\_\_*S*\_\_ 1. Human relations personnel say humor is a choice attribute.
Human relations personnel think a sense of humor is important.

\_\_\_\_\_ 2. Humor provides a non-threatening way for an employee to communicate.
Employees are not threatened by jokes about themselves.

\_\_\_\_\_ 3. Humor oils the wheels of the workplace by providing perspective.
Humor gives you a different viewpoint, which makes things easier at work.

\_\_\_\_\_ 4. At the moment we experience humor, feelings like depression dissolve.
Whenever we laugh, we feel happier.

\_\_\_\_\_ 5. A few moments of humor at work can lead to increased productivity.
Employees with a sense of humor usually work harder.

Relating reading to personal experience

**D** **Answer these questions.**

1. Do you think a sense of humor can help you succeed at work? Why or why not?
2. In what other places is a sense of humor helpful?
3. How can you make your workplace or classroom more fun?

# Three comedians

### Jerry Seinfeld

1    My friends just had a baby. There is so much pressure to see this baby. Every time I talk to them, they say, "You have got to see the baby. When are you coming over to see the baby? See the baby. See the baby."

2    Nobody ever wants you to come over and see their grandfather. "You gotta see him. He's sooo cute. A hundred and sixty-eight pounds, four ounces. I love when they're this age. He's a thousand months. You know the mid-eighties is such a good time for grandpeople. You've got to see him."

3    What's tough about seeing people when they have a new baby is that you have to try and match their level of enthusiasm. They're always so excited. "What do you think of him? What do you think?"

4    Just once I would like to meet a couple that goes, "You know, we're not that happy with him, frankly. I think we really made a big mistake. We should've gotten an aquarium. You want him? We've really had enough."

### Bill Cosby

1    We parents so often blow the business of raising kids, but not because we violate any philosophy of child raising. I doubt there can *be* a philosophy about something so difficult, something so downright mystical, as raising kids. A baseball manager has learned a lot about his job from having played the game, but a parent has not learned a thing from having once been a child. What can you learn about a business in which the child's favorite response is "I don't know"?

2    A father enters his son's room and sees that the boy is missing his hair.

3    "What happened to your head?" the father says, beholding his skin-headed son. "Did you get a haircut?"

4    "I don't know," the boy replies.

5    "You don't *know* if you got a haircut? Well, tell me this: Was your head with you all day?"

6    "I don't know," says the boy.

### Ray Romano

1    My first encounter with a two-year-old came after I had gotten married and become an uncle to my wife's nephew.

2    Until that day I wasn't really that informed about the two-year-old. Oh, I'd read about them, and occasionally I'd see documentaries on the Discovery Channel showing two-year-olds in the wild, where they belong.

3    But my new nephew was the first one I had seen up close. And let me tell you: If you're ever out on a safari and come across one like this, stay in the Jeep.

4    My wife hates when I start talking about him like this.

5    "He's your nephew. You should love him."

6    I'm not saying I don't love him. I just don't want him *in my house*.

7    Why can't I love him from afar? That's how I want to love him – through pictures and folklore.

Adapted from *SeinLanguage, Fatherhood,* and *Everything and a Kite*.

## Before you read

Predicting

A *punch line* is the last part of a joke or story that makes it funny. Read the following punch lines from three comedians. Then answer the question in the box.

1. Just once I would like to meet a couple that goes, "You know, we're not that happy with him, frankly. I think we really made a big mistake. We should've gotten an aquarium. You want him? We've really had enough."
2. "You don't *know* if you got a haircut? Well, tell me this: Was your head with you all day?" "I don't know," says the boy.
3. Why can't I love him from afar? That's how I want to love him – through pictures and folklore.

What subject do you think all three anecdotes have in common?

## Reading

Scanning

Scan the text to check your prediction. Then read the whole text.

## After you read

Understanding main ideas

**A** How would the comedians summarize their complaints? Complete the sentences.

1. Jerry Seinfeld would say to his _friends_ ,
   "I don't want to _see your baby_ !"
2. Bill Cosby would say to his _____ ,
   "I don't want you to say '_____ '!"
3. Ray Romano would say to his _____ ,
   "I don't want our nephew _____ !"

Making inferences

**B** Circle the answer that is *not* true.

1. What does Seinfeld claim parents say about their babies?
   a. how much they weigh
   b. how hard it is to take care of them
   c. what they have learned to do
2. Why does Cosby think parents have problems raising kids?
   a. They have the wrong philosophy.
   b. They've forgotten their own childhood.
   c. Raising children is not easy.
3. Why was Romano surprised when he first met his two-year-old nephew?
   a. The only two-year-olds he had seen were on TV programs about animals.
   b. He didn't know anything about two-year-old children.
   c. His nephew was different from other two-year-olds he knew.

Relating reading to personal experience

**C** Answer these questions.

1. Which anecdote did you think was the funniest? Why?
2. Do you think the subject is humorous? Why or why not?
3. Have you ever watched any of the comedians in the reading perform comedy? If so, did you think they were funny? Why or why not?

## Vocabulary expansion

**A** A Write each idiom in the box next to the correct meaning.

*be in hysterics*             *have someone in stitches*       *almost die laughing*

*stop oneself from laughing*   *laugh out loud*                 *laugh your head off*

*burst out laughing*           *crack people up*                *roar with laughter*

1. not laugh          _____

2. begin laughing     _____

3. laugh a lot         _____ , _____

                       _____ , _____

4. make someone laugh  _____ , _____

**B** Complete each dialog with an idiom from exercise A. Be sure to use the correct word form. (Note: In some cases, more than one answer is possible.)

1. A: How was the movie?
   B: It was really funny. All of the people in the audience were _laughing_
      _their heads off_ .

2. A: What are you laughing about?
   B: My favorite stand-up comic was on TV. He always _____ me
      _____ .

3. A: I'm so embarrassed!
   B: Why? What happened?
   A: I went onstage to give a speech, and I dropped all my notes. Everybody
      _____ .

4. A: My new coworker is really funny.
   B: In what way?
   A: Whenever he tells a joke, everybody _____ ; even the most serious
      person can't _____ .

## Humor and you

Tell your classmates a joke. Then vote for the funniest joke as a class. Discuss why you found the joke funny.

# Acknowledgments

## Illustration credits

Matt Collins        **2, 44, 54**

Ray Alma        **4, 36, 62, 82**

William Waitzman        **50, 68, 94, 98, 101**

David Rolfe        **6, 38**

Dan Vasconcellos        **66, 92, 110, 122**

## Photographic credits

**10**    (top) Getty; (middle, bottom) FoodPix

**14**    Roger Wood/Corbis

**18**    Spencer Grant/Photo Edit

**20**    Jon Freeman/Getty Images

**22**    Bettmann/Corbis

**26**    (both) Getty Images

**28**    (left to right) Steve Azzara/Corbis Sygma; Haruyosi Yamaguchi/Corbis Sygma

**30**    AP/Wide World Photo

**42**    Walter Smith/Corbis

**46**    David Young-Wolff/Photo Edit

**52**    Veer

**58**    Spencer Grant/Photo Edit

**60**    Creatas

**74**    Lawrence Schwartzwald/Corbis Sygma

**76**    David Koskas/Corbis Sygma

**78**    Karen Thomas/Stock, Boston Inc./Picture Quest

**84**    R.P. Kingston/Index Stock

**86**    Farrell Grehan/Corbis

**90**    Julia Waterlow; Eye Ubiquitous/Corbis

**100**    Pat Doyle/Corbis

**102**    Creatas

**106**    AP/Wide World Photo

**108**    Paul A. Souders/Corbis

**116**    Courtesy of Renzo Piano

**117**    (left to right) Courtesy of Renzo Piano; Courtesy of Kendrick Bangs Kellogg; Courtesy of Bart Prince; Courtesy of Douglas Cardinal

**118**    Tim Boyle/Getty Images

**124**    Getty Images

**126**    (top to bottom) David Turnley/Corbis; Bettmann/Corbis; Steve Azzara/Corbis

# Text credits

The authors and publishers are grateful for permission to reprint the following items:

90  From "Shaolin Temple Journal; Where Zen and Kung Fu Got Off to a Flying Start," by Erik Eckholm, *The New York Times*, March 28, 1998, Section A, page 4. Copyright © 1998 by The New York Times Co. Reprinted with permission.

92  Adapted from "The Karate Generation," by Susan H. Greenberg, *Newsweek*, August 28, 2000, 136, no. 9, page 50. Copyright © 2000 Newsweek, Inc. All rights reserved. Reprinted by permission.

94  From IRON AND SILK by Mark Salzman, copyright © 1986 by Mark Salzman. Used by permission of Random House, Inc.

98  Adapted from "Smart Clothes" by Louise Marks. From the website http://www.usc.edu/isd.publications/networker/97-98/Nov_Dec_97/dispatch-smart_clothes.html. Copyright © 1999 Information Services Division, University of Southern California.

100 Article by Miki Takashima from *The Daily Yomiuri*, October 20, 2001. Copyright © The Daily Yomiuri. Reprinted with permission.

102 Adapted from "How To Separate Trends from Fads," by Irma Zandl, *Brandweek*, October 23, 2000, © 2003 VNU BUSINESS MEDIA INC. Used with permission from *Brandweek*.

106 Adapted from "Media: Alien concepts: Something strange is happening to US tabloids. They are trying to upmarket," by Edward Helmore, *The Guardian* (London), October 9, 2000, Media Pages, page 10.

108 From "When our worlds collide," by Richard Folkers, *U.S. News & World Report*, Vol. 123, September 15, 1997, page 40. Copyright 1997 U.S. News & World Report, L.P. Reprinted with permission.

110 From VIEWING VIOLENCE: HOW MEDIA VIOLENCE AFFECTS YOUR CHILD AND ADOLESCENT by Madeline Levine, copyright © 1996 by Madeline Levine. Used by permission of Doubleday, a division of Random House, Inc.

114 From GIRL WITH A PEARL EARRING by Tracy Chevalier, copyright © 1999 by Tracy Chevalier. Used by permission of Plume, an imprint of Penguin Group (USA) Inc. Reprinted by permission of HarperCollins Publishers Ltd. (London) © 1999 Tracy Chevalier.

116 Adapted from "The missing link: Architects have discovered the Holy Grail of building design – organics," by Maria Cook, *The Ottawa Citizen*, March 17, 2002, page C8.

118 Adapted from "How forgeries corrupt our top museums," by Peter Watson, *New Statesman* (London), December 2000 – January 2001, 129, pages 14 – 15. This is taken from an article which first appeared in *New Stateman*.

122 Adapted from "So Who's The Comedian? 120 Terrifying Seconds in The Spotlight at the Improv," by Gene Weingarten, *The Washington Post*, September 14, 1999, page C01. Copyright © 1999, *The Washington Post*. Reprinted with permission.

124 Adapted from "Taking Humor Seriously in the Workplace," by Steven Sultanoff. From the website http://www.humormatters.com/articles/workplace.htm.

126 Adapted from *SeinLanguage*, by Jerry Seinfeld, © 1993 by Jerry Seinfeld, Bantam Books, page 63. And *Everything And A Kite*, by Ray Romano, © 1998 Luckykids, Inc., page 89. And *Fatherhood*, by Bill Cosby © 1986 by William H. Cosby, Jr., Dolphin Book (Doubleday and Company, Inc.) page 20.